Memoirs
of a
Mexican Politician

Memoirs of a Mexican Politician

Roderic A. Camp

Illustrations by Lawrence Mills

University of New Mexico Press
Albuquerque

To Christopher and Alexander

Design by Milenda Nan Ok Lee

Illustrations © by Lawrence Mills

Library of Congress Cataloging-in-Publication Data

Camp, Roderic Ai.
  Memoirs of a Mexican politician.

  1. Mexico—History—20th century—Fiction.   I. Title.
PS3553.A4376M4   1988   813'.54   87-30244
ISBN 0-8263-1041-9
ISBN 0-8263-1042-7 (pbk.)

Contents

Contents

Introduction

The impetus for this book really begins some twenty years ago when at the age of nineteen I ventured to Mexico on my own. Living with a family in Mexico City for a year, walking through the streets for many miles each weekend, and travelling to farther points by bus and train during breaks, I became attached to the country—its history, its culture, and its people. As time passed, and my dreamer's avocation became my profession, I saw more clearly the harsh realities of Mexico's development. Still, in spite of the objectivity social science attempts to instill among its practitioners, I have not shed a special curiosity about the past and present, and most importantly, about the lives of Mexicans who themselves saw the twists and turns followed by their country on its road to progress.

Knowing that nothing substitutes for a personal view of history, I frequently interviewed a friend of the señorita who owned the home in which I lived. Her age, which gave her a view of Mexico extending back to the Porfiriato, combined with her natural talents as a raconteur, allowed her to regale me with fascinating stories from the Revolution of 1910. Those conversations were the first of many interviews with Mexicans of all backgrounds and professions, for I am one of those curious North Americans who likes to speak with cab drivers, porters, and the ordinary man or woman on the street.

In 1969, while engaged in my dissertation research, I began to correspond with and later interview men and women at all levels of Mexican public life. Having continued these activities for the last fifteen years, the letters and interviews now extend into the hundreds. I have interviewed public officials ranging from presidents of Mexico to ordinary department heads. Although interviewing Mexican political leaders is not unique, the length, breadth, and time covered by my interviews has been most unusual. Recognizing that I had in my files an original and rare source of information, several years ago I asked myself how it might be published. I had used some of this information in my professional research, and most particularly, it forms the basis for my work on the socialization of Mexican political leaders, published in Mexico and the United States.

However, I was not wholly satisfied with confining my interview information to monographic studies. Much of it has a value of an anecdotal nature and, while not germane to most formal scholarship, when put together in a coherent fashion could be quite revealing about the milieu of the Mexican political culture. Moreover, I wanted to bring political history alive to the North American student by approaching it from a different perspective. Intrigued with the possibilities, I began, as part of my other research interests, to read autobiographies by prominent Mexican figures in public life published since the 1930s. Further, more information became available through oral history interviews, pioneered in Mexico in the 1960s by Professor James W. Wilkie.

Concurrent with my research interests I have long been concerned with the availability of teaching materials on Latin

Introduction

America. I have found, along with my colleagues at other institutions, that there is a scarcity of materials in English, from a Latin American viewpoint, that deal with political life. With that need in mind, I have sought in this work to combine first-hand knowledge of Mexican political life as told to me by politicians themselves or as revealed in their memoirs.

The central figure of this work—Antonio Gutiérrez—is a composite of politicians who grew up during the last decade of the Profiriato, were educated during the second and third decade of this century, and dominated political life from 1940 to 1970. I choose to have him come from Michoacán, a state in west central Mexico, because many politicians from this region, in this generation, gained access to important positions. While the individual is fictional, the events in his life are true, as told to me by a select group of prominent politicians, and only the places and times have been altered. I have also placed these events in their correct historical context and, as the reader will see, actual historical figures are interspersed throughout the story. Their lives are briefly detailed in a biographical glossary, enabling the reader to grasp the larger historical context.

Stylistically this book combines the typical features and emphases most prominent in Mexican political memoirs, along with dialog and fictional transitions. It is similar to the work of the late Oscar Lewis in that it lets the author, in this case, a Mexican politician, speak for himself, without my intervention. In doing so this work takes on all of the stylistic conventions, both good and bad, of the typical Mexican political autobiography. Further, my friend and colleague, Lawrence Mills, has graciously used his imagination and years of travel in Mexico to capture visually many of the images within these pages. Thus this book, both in format and content, attempts to accurately mirror the recollections of political elites, or what Wilkie has aptly labelled "elitelore."

Introduction

Mexican autobiographies, though, are not as revealing as those written by most European and North American politicians. Their style is straightforward and rather dry. They divulge very little that is personal about the author, especially about his family and his wife and children. Typically, most politicians reveal more about their parents and their school days than any other period in their lives. Both the style and content, which this memoir remains faithful to, are revealing about characteristics of Mexico's political culture. Although some Mexicans, like José Vasconcelos, will include anecdotes about a wife and a mistress simultaneously, this is a rarity in most Mexican memoirs.

Naturally Mexican autobiographies also tend to gloss over political corruption, unless it can be attributed to a political enemy, or make the author appear in a better light. But even with these exceptions, it is a topic few want to discuss concretely, let alone put to paper in a memoir. In part, their reluctance is self-protecting since the more tight-mouthed each politician is about the system, the same one which has nurtured all successful leaders since 1929, the more positive their ambience can be viewed.

Many themes and interpretations emphasized by this generation appear in Antonio Gutiérrez's recollections. It is useful to highlight these for the novice reader of Mexican politics. As Gutiérrez reveals, he was a youngster during the apex of Mexico's Revolution of 1910, which was the most destructive twentieth-century event in the Western Hemisphere. Over a million Mexicans died during the decade between 1910 and 1920. The violence generated by the Revolution, however, occurred unevenly throughout Mexico. In some regions there was constant upheaval and fighting, in others, the events only indirectly touched the lives of local residents. But for many working- and middle-class Mexicans, the Revolution heightened their interest in politics. In the 1920s, more Mexicans became aware of national as distinct from local concerns. The trainman young Antonio meets on his trip to Mexico City exemplifies this changed Mexican.

Antonio represents the modern politician whose entire career hinges on an exceptional access to education. Contrary to earlier expectations, the Revolution did not increase upward social mobility, at least in political life, for an extended period of time. Antonio, from a lower-class provincial background, is part of that generation in the 1920s which briefly had access to those opportunities that provide the necessary credentials and experiences for a successful political career. His father's generation had very little formal education. But those politicians from humble origins who succeed in overcoming their class background do so because of the strong support given to them by a parent or parents, often their mother. Many members of this generation, similar to Antonio, are fatherless or even orphans at a young age. A persevering parent, or grandparent, is a regular feature in the successful politician's background.

The early lives of Antonio's generation were characterized by an admirable simplicity. Material goods were few. Communications, physical and intellectual, were slow. The provinces were isolated from Mexico City. Yet, people like Antonio's father, with a modicum of education, were curious about the outside world. Some travelled; others read. Mexican rural life wasn't stagnant before the Revolution. Change was afoot, but the pace was slow.

The successful politician was imbued with two crucial qualities by his parents: will and curiosity. Young men like Antonio and Ramón had to overcome tremendous odds in a society where less than 1 percent of the population entered a university. They had to seek out those opportunities, to seek out knowledge about the world around them. Contrary to myth,

Introduction

politicians of Antonio Gutiérrez's generation were extraordinarily well educated in many respects. Their knowledge was broad. Many of them read Adams, Jefferson, and Lincoln, the great philosophers of Europe, and knew North American history better than we ourselves do. Their appetite for knowledge was insatiable. But that alone was insufficient equipment for survival in the educational and political system. Self-discipline was essential. This was a goal-oriented generation. They gave up a lot, for themselves and for Mexico.

Antonio's friends saw Mexico's future as wide open in the 1920s. There was nowhere to go but up. They were excited by the possibilities, not just of fulfilling personal ambitions, but also of serving as the engineers who would restructure all aspects of Mexican life. The Revolution left them a clean slate. They wanted to rebuild Mexico in their own image. They reeked of optimism. This positive outlook was infectious. As they matured they would be the generation that took Mexico out of the period of post-revolutionary violence and instability characteristic of the 1920s and 1930s, and into the era of peace after 1940.

The impact of revolutions on cultural behavior seems overrated. Cultural patterns in Mexico's political life, well established in the nineteenth century, and earlier, continued to persist. The tenor of Mexican politics retained a natural continuity from one era to the next. For Antonio's generation the key socializing experience was passing through preparatory school and the university, most commonly in law, in a post-revolutionary society. For these future politicians, political participation in their student years prepared them for national politics. Some, who joined opposition candidates' campaigns, became disillusioned with public life, never to return to active politics. Others, who learned from bitter experience, recognized the influence and power exercised by a revolutionary political elite and attached themselves to their ranks as young protégés. Like most of us, they thought they could alter the system from within.

Throughout a Mexican politician's career, especially if he or she is successful, is a constant search for companions one can trust. Antonio's generation came to rely heavily on early friends, usually from school. At first, geography characterized their contacts. But as they moved from the provinces to Mexico City, they brushed shoulders with Mexicans from all regions of the country and from all walks of life. The leading schools acted like a larger mixer, homogenizing a generation of Mexicans who would lead their society.

But as Antonio soon learned from his political experiences, the Revolution hadn't destroyed the tendency to examine political issues and personalities with a lack of objectivity. Many still were polarized in their views, and certain interpretations were repressed. Furthermore, major personalities dominated political life both regionally and nationally. Mexicans tended to offer their loyalties to strong figures like General Múgica, rather than necessarily identifying with a given ideological bent. Often, friendship, not ideas, became the crucial cement in linking the political fortunes of Mexican public figures. Antonio, for example, joins a significant student strike, more out of loyalty to his companions than for any commitment to the goals of the strikers.

However, Antonio's generation, at least collectively, believed they held a shared ideology. One of their repeated concerns was the importance of the Constitution of 1917 as a benchmark for political life. For them, the constitution needed to be institutionalized, especially when it came to replacing military leaders who controlled national politics with a civilian counterpart. For others, the issue of the supremacy of state over Church is also tied to this document as part of their revolutionary heritage. The goals of the Constitution highlighted the bitterness of Antonio's generation toward the election results of 1927 and 1929. Yet, their hopes about democracy and effective participation have not yet been translated into a reality for Mexico.

For most Mexicans of Antonio's generation, political mentors were professors at the National Preparatory School, or its provincial equivalent, and the National University or state public institutions. These part-time teachers, many of whom were successful public figures, used the classroom to recruit Mexico's future leaders. Miguel Alemán, Mexico's president from 1946 to 1952 and in this story Antonio's most successful companion, institutionalizes this student-professor relationship in politics. Most of his cabinet are former professors and student friends.

The migration of politicians and other Mexicans to Mexico City has numerous consequences. One of the more important is the urbanization of Mexico's governmental elite. Their shared experiences have contributed to Mexico's stability and continuity in leadership, but have also generated a somewhat parochial or insular view of national issues and problems. The Church-state conflict during this era, for example, was critical to social life in many parts of Mexico. Yet, although initiated by the national government, the students were insulated from its more important effects in Mexico City.

Antonio realizes later than many of his companions that, if he wants to guide his country's future, the private sector is not the route to take. Ultimately, he not only sees politics as the most appropriate vehicle but also realizes that to have any impact at all, he must join the political establishment. Once in public life, he quickly learns that personal contacts are the key to success, just as they are in Mexico's private sector. Indeed, personal ties between government and the private sector have enhanced the careers of businessmen, too. Each politician must develop a cohesive, dynamic pool of supporters, an *equipo* or team, as the Mexicans call it, and they must attach themselves to a larger clique, or *camarilla*, of ambitious, upwardly mobile politicians led by a personality higher up on the political ladder.

Gutiérrez realizes from his first success in national politics, with his nomination as a congressman from his home district, that government leadership designates candidates for the Institutional Revolutionary Party and its antecedents. Federal deputies, we soon learn, do not rely on a tie to their constituency, either to obtain the nomination, or to go on to other posts. The Chamber of Deputies is devoid of the power which Congress exercises in the United States. Primarily, the deputy serves to represent individuals and groups from his district in the labyrinth of Mexico's national bureaucracy. Mexico's official party operates in some respects like the old patronage system in the United States, reminiscent of the Democratic Party machine in Chicago. Others variables play a role too, among them the media. The press has not, nor does it today, function with the same guidelines as the print media in the United States. Political careers are promoted by journalists paid to give favorable press coverage to individual personalities or agencies.

Political careers for Antonio's generation are not strictly consecutive. These individuals alternate between public posts and their professions, often taking on part- or full-time positions in academia. When Gutiérrez enters the world of state gubernatorial politics, he learns again how the nomination process is dominated by the center, and often by the very apex of the Mexican political system, the president. But even when a Mexican politician is in a position of considerable authority, he often lacks control over his subordinates. As Antonio tragically exiences, lower-echelon officials often abuse their authority, sometimes in the belief that they are obeying the wishes of a superior.

Many Mexicans believe that an individual holding an executive office, whether as governor, cabinet member, or president, is fully in control. But even for the president, and much more so for lesser figures, politics is a game of reciprocity. In all of his positions Antonio learns you need to give up something to obtain something else. Your skill at acquiring support and cultivating friends is not only critical to advancement within the system, but also in securing the funds to implement your programs. Whereas the President cannot physically control the political system, if he abuses his authority, he risks destroying it.

In the 1980s, many of the survivors of Gutiérrez's generation, in their seventies and eighties, have lost their optimism. They are living in the society their leadership helped to produce. Many feel a distance from the present generation, which they believe is sometimes misguided in its goals and lacking in the skills to govern Mexico. To Antonio's generation, Mexico's government is plagued by an ever-growing bureaucracy unresponsive to the needs of ordinary Mexicans. They have begun to raise questions about the size of the state relative to the private sector.

As in all autobiographies, one has to read between the lines, understanding that the writer may wish the reader to accept his view of an event without question. Mexican memoirs are limited in their political insight by the secrecy surrounding the decision-making process, and by the fact that so many decisions stem from the President himself. It's very difficult, even for politicians of the inner circle, to suggest motivations for decisions affecting his career, or those of others. Often, they just aren't known. This work accurately reflects these deficiencies. Still, for the wary reader, much can be learned about the Mexican politician in the fictionalized memoir that follows.

Roderic A. Camp

Acknowledgment

This is a book which I have had in my mind for many years. It has gone through many versions, and I would like to thank Emily Ellen Camp and Roger O. Camp for their criticisms and suggestions. Also, I am indebted to David Holtby for his enthusiasm and interest, and to Antonio Martínez Báez for a Mexican perspective.

Part One

My Village
1905 – 1915

I was a Mexican of ordinary circumstances like the majority of my generation. I worked hard, and through many good turns of fortune, my life followed paths which only a few have taken. Whether my contributions in public life, and I am proud of them, have been better or worse than the next man's, I leave to historians to decide. Instead, I have penned these words in the hopes that my children and grandchildren, and those who only knew the post-Revolutionary years from textbooks, will hear firsthand the efforts of my generation to build a new Mexico, a heritage of challenges for the years to come. I dedicate these words to my saintly mother and grandmother, who with courage and sacrifice, made possible the life I describe in the following pages.

—Lic. Antonio Gutiérrez Enríquez

1

Purépero

My earliest memory of my native village must date from
around 1912 when I was about seven. It was morning and my
grandmother sent me to the store for some eggs. It had rained
heavily the night before; a thick mist hung over the dull white-
washed buildings with their waist-high pastel trims pocked
and peeling. The soles of my feet slapped the smooth cobble-
stones, and my feet slid in my sandals with each crossing of
the irregular gulleys and valleys still draining the night's rain.
When some of the dirty water standing in the low places seeped
into my sandals, the hemp straps rubbed and irritated my skin.

As I rounded the corner and entered a wider street, the sun
broke through the early mist, warming me. The street sloped
gradually and ended two blocks farther in the town plaza. To
the side was an unpainted cement trough full of rainwater,
and the broken red tiles in the square were shaded by a circle
of alamo trees, touching each other as though to form a fence.
Except for several wagons, the plaza appeared deserted. I
shivered as the sun disappeared behind a thick cloud, and I
hurried to the end of the street. As I approached the square, I

3

could see Señora Gálvez, who, with her husband, operated the small store. It was typical of most family stores in the countryside then and now. From a small clay jug, she sprinkled water across the hard-packed earth beneath the arcade. Grabbing a short-handled broom, lopsided with wear, she swept the debris and loose dirt into a narrow ditch beyond the covered entrance. I crossed the square, trailing mud behind me. I jumped across the open drainage ditch and caught Señora Gálvez's eye.

"My grandmother asked me to buy six eggs," I said shyly.

Señora Gálvez smiled and leaned the broom against the weathered lintel. As she went behind the counter, I reached to my waist, untying the half-knot from the drawstring of a small hemp bag. I laid the bag on the countertop, while Señora Gálvez selected the eggs from a large, cracked porcelain bowl on the shelf in a darkened corner.

"Here you are child," she said, placing each egg carefully in the bag. In my left hand, I clutched a colorful, silk handkerchief containing several coins. I gave her the money and she gave me one small coin in return, which I wrapped in the handkerchief and tucked into my pocket. I gently took my bag, making sure not to let the eggs tumble against each other or the countertop. Money was for necessities only. I had already learned its value to us. To lose the few coins I carried meant we couldn't buy food for an entire day. As a child, the responsibility thrust on me quickly turned me into a young adult in many ways. I remember to this day being very methodical and careful about carrying food and money. I thanked Señora Gálvez, and she asked me to pass on her greetings to my grandmother and mother.

As I crossed the square, the sun shone brightly. The moisture from the rain combined with the refuse in the ditch and gave off a rich odor. When I reached the far street, I noticed a column of men, led by a light-skinned man atop a black, mud-spattered horse. Partly hidden by an alamo tree, I peered

around the trunk and recognized the men as soldiers, dressed in unpressed khaki. Several had identical belts of bleached webbing, while others wore something similar to my piece of rope. Mud caked their boots. Occasionally a piece would shake loose, to fall among the stones or to be picked up by the heel of the man next in line. At first, they appeared to be in a straight file, but as they marched closer, I could see the column resembled a straggling line of schoolchildren. Their Indian faces masked their emotions as they mechanically set their feet down in time with the hooves of the horse. Most carried rifles on their shoulders, although the last two did not seem to have any weapons, their hands swinging freely from their sides. As they approached the square, the man on the horse shouted, "Patrol, halt!" The men came to a stumbling stop.

The officer slowly turned his horse at right angles with his troop; the saddle creaked as he twisted his body and straightened his back.

"Sergeant. Have one of the recruits water my horse and give the men a rest. Over there," he commanded with a wave of his hand in the direction of where I stood.

Startled by his movement, I scurried home, eager to tell of my first view of government soldiers. Contrary to the view most young people today have of the revolutionary period, not every town or region was unsettled by the violence. Certain parts were relatively untouched by the upheaval of the period. My village had not been outwardly disturbed by the Revolution, although the Federals frequently conscripted recruits from Tarascan descendents in outlying areas. For me, the Revolution hardly rippled the surface of my tranquil and happy life. I hurried up the street and eventually came to our door and, lifting the latch gingerly, stepped into the shadow and closed the door behind me.

2

Grandmother

My father died when I was three. One of eleven children, he had worked the fields with his father since childhood, growing the traditional Mexican crops of chili, beans, and corn. He had only two years of schooling but, determined to improve his lot in life, he apprenticed himself to a harness-maker. After years of perfecting his skills, he established his own shop and became moderately successful. He also taught himself to read and write, both of which helped him in his business. To learn about the world beyond his village, he traveled several times to Morelia, the social and political capital of our state. Once, when he was twenty-one, he traveled to Mexico City to sell his wares in the central market. I never heard my father talk about this visit, but I listened with awe to the stories my grandmother told about his experiences and impressions from that trip.

Despite our simple way of life, and the limited resources we had available, my grandmother always seemed to me to be a person superior to her circumstances. She commonly dressed in dark clothing, often black, but her appearance was garnished with a black mantilla typical of a Spanish lady, which she wore carefully on her gray hair. A tortoise comb from Veracruz locked her hair in a tightly wrapped bun. Under her left sleeve she kept one of her colorful handkerchiefs, allowing an inch or so of one corner to hang below the gathered end. Though many of her clothes were threadbare and shiny in places from wear, her demeanor was such that she was still a striking figure even in her sixties.

Grandmother moved to the adobe stove, adding several more pieces of charcoal to the small blaze under the griddle of dull, black iron. As she splashed water over the surface, I watched how it separated into dirty, gray balls and danced away with a sizzle. She took the eggs from the bag I had brought back from the store, setting them aside for a special casserole of spinach, a dish she had learned from cooking in a large hotel in Morelia during her youth.

She flapped a tortilla down upon the griddle and exclaimed, "Well, Toño, we will soon have several warm ones to take the chill from your bones." The corn puffed up as the tortilla filled with hot air, and Grandmother mashed the center down with her fingers. Grandmother flipped the tortilla over, burning some spots and toasting others.

Hesitant at first, but growing more excited as I talked, I described the soldiers I had seen. Grandmother asked me how many there were and I told her many.

"Did they have uniforms?" she asked.

"Oh yes, and they wore boots too! Do you think they're from Mexico City?" I asked.

"Well, possibly," Grandmother reasoned, "but it is more likely that they are from the local garrison."

Not content with her answer, I asked, "How far away is Mexico City?"

"Mexico City," she sighed, pausing. "Oh, many miles, Grandson. I have never been there myself, but your father traveled there and brought me back a beautiful pair of boots with many buttons up the front." Once she took them out of a small chest and let me stick my feet in them, although she wouldn't allow me to trudge around imitating an adult. I remember the feel of the soft, smooth leather, just like a pair of women's gloves.

The aroma of tortillas cooking filled the room. My nostrils cherished the smell and my stomach rumbled impatiently. I had distracted my grandmother with my questions; suddenly, she snatched the over-cooked tortilla from the oven and laid it on a small plate. With good humor, she promised to give it to me after it had cooled.

Tilting her forehead upward, as if to read something on the ceiling, she paused then said, "When your father was still by himself, he had a small harness shop on Calle Malagón. He was very interested in his country, and read the paper *El Monitor Comercial*, which came irregularly from Morelia. Because many of the events described in the paper occurred in Mexico City, he decided to go there. Your compadre, Señor Romero, was sending a wagon to Morelia to pick up some bolts of material for his tailor shop. Taking a number of harnesses with him, plus some money he had saved from his business, your father traveled to Morelia in the wagon. By paying a small fare, he traveled the highway between Morelia and Mexico, arriving after many days journey."

Wanting her to go on, I asked, "And what did Papa say the city looked like?"

She had told me various versions of this story before, but she embellished each new account in such a way that my interest never lagged.

She continued, "There was a cathedral that was so large, it was greater than the entire plaza of our village, and taller than the highest tree. The bells sang louder than a village band at a wedding celebration. The walls were of great pieces of stone,

11

thick enough to protect the riches surrounding the saints from those who would do them harm."

My grandmother, as was true of most of her generation, was extremely religious. She never missed a mass at our local church. My mother attended fairly regularly, too, and of course I went along. But after the age of twelve, without parental supervision, my religious interest, which had never been anything but superficial, waned. The ceremonies seemed all too solemn. Unlike my grandmother, I could not visualize the great works of art, religious or otherwise. For me, the secular world seemed exciting.

"And the carriages," I interjected, "what did he say about them?"

"A great street led into the center of the city. So large was this street—," she spread her hands wide apart—"that it contained many parks in its center. There strolled ladies with white ruffled umbrellas and men in black suits; carriages, of all shades and sizes, filled this great avenue."

"Did he ride the machine on wheels?" I wanted to know.

"Oh yes," she continued. "Mixed in among the wagons were even larger wagons. These had roofs and were pulled along two grooves in the street by horses. I think your father called them trolleys."

By then, Grandmother had cooked three more tortillas, two of which she gave to me. I rolled them loosely in my nimble fingers, making a crude spoon at one end for dipping into some sauce. I ate my tortillas, and excitedly, my mouth full, asked her how long he stayed.

She paused, then replied that he had become very interested in the city and, since he was unmarried with no family to support, had decided to stay for awhile and work. "He had not brought his leather tools with him, so after selling his harnesses, he worked carrying water for a group of men at San Lázaro, a place in Mexico where the trains arrive."

"Just like the pictures in my book?"

"Yes child, I think so, but I've never seen a train either. I remember my mother describing how frightened she was when this smoking, noisy machine first passed near her village, going from Veracruz to Mexico many years ago. It's made entirely of iron, and the wheels travel on shiny, metal rails, held to the ground by huge nails and large planks of wood."

I remember telling her that someday I would like to ride a train. She said I would.

From the darkened doorway of our other small room, I heard a soft whimpering noise. My little sister had awakened. The bed creaked as my mother shifted her legs to attend to the child. She would nurse the baby before coming out to share breakfast with us.

3

Mama

Mama was a remarkable woman. Born in Apatzingan, she moved to Morelia as a young child. There, through the efforts of the woman who employed her father, she received a complete education from the Academia de Niñas of Morelia, a forerunner of the normal school located in the capital during those years. Then, of course, such an education was a remarkable achievement for the child of any peasant or worker, and for a girl, it was even more unusual.

Father met Mama while on one of his trips to Morelia. They were introduced by relatives. Father, by then almost a confirmed bachelor, was impressed with her beauty and an inquisitiveness unusual for her sex and age. He married her after a brief courtship and brought her back to Purépero.

I can hardly recall them together, but I believe they were quite happy, and still much in love when my father died shortly before the birth of my sister Camila. Mama never quite recovered from his death, and although still young and robust, she never remarried. Her education was to be a godsend, for through her knowledge, she sustained our family, and strongly influenced my life. After the death of my father, she, with the help of Señor Romero, sold the harnesses and tools to an ambitious man who hoped to follow the same path of apprenticeship as my father. He paid for these goods in installments, providing my mother with a small income while she decided how she would support her son and an unborn child. Soon after the birth of my sister, Grandmother came to live with us, freeing my mother of the need to stay at home and care for her children.

In my youth I never realized how many children were orphans or had lost a parent as infants. My circumstances, in that respect, were not unique for my generation. Many of my contemporaries lost a parent, generally a father. Life expectancy was low, and of course the disease and violence of the Revolution itself increased the likelihood of such an early and devastating loss. My own mother was instrumental in my formation; but I am convinced, if my friends are an accurate measure of similar circumstances, that many prominent figures owe their achievements to a self-sacrificing mother rather than to a father.

Although she had no previous teaching experience, Mama decided to open a private school. Those who were able to—tradesmen and some of the more prosperous muleteers—paid a reasonable weekly fee for giving their children the rudiments of a primary education. By the time I was four, I too accompanied my mother to the small, single-room building provided by one parent in lieu of his fee. She started out with seven students, but by the time I was five, the number had increased to fifteen. The books were secondhand, and bought by Señor Romero in Morelia. Mama paid for them by saving money on our basic necessities. In this way, I had access to stories and pictures of city life not seen by most children of my background.

My Village, 1905–1915

To this day I remember Mama coming through the narrow doorway. The light from the kitchen window crossed her face, illuminating the sparkle in her eyes as she spoke.

"Ay, boy," she said, half scolding me, "always asking your grandmother questions. What a curious mind you have, even for a little one."

I admitted the truth of her accusation, and told her that Grandmother had been telling me about Papa's trip to Mexico City. She asked me if I had finished breakfast and told me to go wash the sleep from my eyes and comb my hair for school.

Mother and Grandmother conversed as I crossed to the rear of our cooking area and unlatched our rickety backdoor. I swung the door shut behind me and stepped into the narrow, enclosed yard. It was surrounded by walls made of stones. They had once been filled and smoothed over with adobe, which had long since washed away. The top of the wall was irregular, worn down by weather and children's feet.

In one corner stood a large, sprawling sycamore, whose limbs at one point reached the overhang of our roof. This tree shaded a triangular section of the yard, but left the remainder exposed to sunlight for most of the day. Grandmother maintained a small garden of greens and squash, which she tended carefully. The rows were compact, and although planted with no tools or string to measure the distance between rows, they were parallel. From the age of four, I had helped her plant and weed the garden. Because of my age, I saw it as entertainment, rather than work, and constantly asked if I could help maintain the plot. Toward the front of the yard, closest to the back of the house, Grandmother had also planted two small apricot saplings, which she hoped would one day bear fruit.

Once as an adult I travelled to Bolivia. This was just a few years ago. What my house was like then, in the 1910s, was similar to those occupied by the highland Indians of that

17

Part One

Andean country. Latin Americans, including Mexicans, in many places not only use mud and adobe to construct their homes, a product natural to their locale and generally free for the taking, but they share a fetish for enclosing themselves from outside eyes. Years ago I read a book by some missionaries to India entitled *Behind Mud Walls*. Even some Asians protected themselves, their families, and their values in this way, no matter how poor. Perhaps it symbolizes something important about our view of life, of each other, and of society? But in my childhood, it was a wonderful refuge, a place where I could dream and fantasize in tranquility.

Both my mother and my grandmother loved color. The rows of flowers they planted against the back wall contrasted with its faded green. I never knew all the names of the flowers, but I best remember the poinsettia for its brilliant red swatches, and the carnations for their rich fragrance. The garden attracted many birds and insects. In particular I came to admire the agility and grace of the hummingbird, which seasonally feasted on the flowers' nectar. We were fortunate to have several pairs nesting nearby, and during the mating season, I would hear the telltale zoom of their wings as they performed fantastic aeronautic feats, diving like miniature bombers, pulling up inches short of whatever object served as their target as they carried out U-shaped flight patterns.

Flies pestered us in the summer and fall, but we enjoyed several varieties of butterflies, among them the monarch. Even as a child, I admired the delicate patterns on its wings, so skillfully painted by nature. Once, I found a deformed butterfly just emerging from its cocoon. I rescued it from the hungry birds. Its wings were twisted and wrinkled, and they could not open fully to allow it to fly. I kept my butterfly for many days in a bowl with flowers and leaves. It would cling tightly to my finger with its fine, black legs, and if I put it on my shoulder, it would hang from the seam of my muslin shirt.

My Village, 1905–1915

One morning, I woke up to find my little friend dead, probably from starvation. I carefully buried it in a small rag among my favorite carnations, close to the fragrance which attracted its brothers.

Near the back door was a small wooden stand. On top stood a large, chipped, clay bowl, which at one time had a distinct pattern glazed on its exterior. Now it couldn't be deciphered. This served as our washbowl. Underneath the stand was a small stool my father had made for me. I pulled it out, stepped up, and cupped my hands letting the cool liquid flow over the top of my palms. It felt good to splash the water on my face, hair, and neck. I reached for the rag hung from a broken peg. I rubbed my face dry, leaving my hair quite wet. I ran a crude, wooden comb, with several missing teeth, through the snarls in my hair. Before placing the comb back on the table, I pulled out the hairs caught at the base of the teeth, letting them fall slowly to the ground below.

We had very few material goods in those days. I sincerely believe that I am not romanticizing my poor childhood, but we did not have a strong desire for the consumer products that overflow the shelves of urban department stores today. I have thought many times over the years that our disinterest in such goods wasn't simply a result of not knowing about them nor was it an indication of blissful poverty. For us, food, a home, good health, and security were far more important than the latest fashion or laborsaving device. Of course, once people have the essential needs, they have time to contemplate abstract interests, including such notions as freedom and dignity. Indeed, our Revolution, according to the historians, was about land and liberty, a material and psychological goal. But which was more important? That will be debated long after these words are written. Probably, no answer will be forthcoming.

Part One

The door unlatched as I finished washing up, and Mother emerged from the darkened kitchen. Her dress was calico; its flowered pattern had faded. She wore a string of lime green glass beads; their color caught the green of her own unusual olive-brown eyes. Her skin was neither brown nor white; its tone was similar to eggshells. A small scar, from a cut in childhood, marred only slightly the smoothness of her arms and hands. Her hair hung in braids, similar to the style worn today by maids in Mexico, accentuating her Indian features.

She asked me if I had washed carefully. I started to tell her all about the soldiers, but she wanted only to give me a moral lesson.

"Life is full of surprises, some pleasant, and some unpleasant. But each morning, try to wake up with a smile as wide as the sun, and a heart as cheerful as the singing birds."

I smiled. Mother, despite her own personal tragedies and hardships, tried very hard to instill in me a sense of hope. Her optimism rubbed off on me, and, if not apparent in my personal behavior, it was to become part of my philosophical outlook. In later life, I could appreciate more the value of this quality. Very few people achieve all they hope to do, whether they follow careers in politics, business, intellectual life, or whatever. I have had the good fortune to know many prominent Mexicans and, despite their many differences, a quality they share is their ability to rebound from failure, personal tragedy, and obstacles to their professional goals. Actually, many individuals have abilities equal or superior to these Mexicans, but they lack the combativeness to sustain themselves against life's hurdles. This is especially true for those members of my generation who came from such humble beginnings. And, it is true today. All of our advances, our modern technology, have not changed the importance of will. Now I understand that. My mother probably could not explain its value but instinctively she knew it was important to me, to my survival.

20

My Village, 1905–1915

After Mama saw I was cleaned up, we got ready to leave for school. My sister stayed at home with my grandmother. I trudged off with Mama and asked her what we would do at school; she explained the day's assignments. After that, I wanted to hear the story of the foolish schoolmaster. As I walked along, holding a fistful of Mama's skirt, she told me one of my favorite stories.

"Once there was a schoolmaster named Pedro de Urdemalas—not the kind of schoolmaster you would want to be. One day Pedro said to his wife, 'I'm going to set up a school.'

'But how can that be?' she exclaimed. 'You can't even read and write.'

'That's none of your business,' the schoolmaster snapped. 'Don't meddle in things you know nothing about.'" I giggled.

"All the villagers sent their children to Pedro's school," Mama continued, "and all they were taught to say was, 'You can't and I can't either.'

After some time had passed, the parents asked their children, 'Let's see. What have you learned in school? What does that writing say?'

'Well, it says, 'You can't, and I can't either,' said one child.

Another child told his father, 'It says, 'But you can't and neither can I.'

'It couldn't say that,' the parent protested.

'Yes, father, that's what the teacher said,'" I laughed aloud. "Once they understood what this strange phrase meant, 'You can't read, and I can't either,' all the villagers got together, and they went to see the famous teacher. But he had disappeared in a cloud of dust along with his wife. And so, the villagers were tricked."*

* Américo Paredes, *Folktales of Mexico* (Chicago: University of Chicago Press, 1970), p. 160.

4

Rosalia

After a walk of several minutes we arrived at a row of buildings; some were occupied by craftsmen, others by families, another was our school. Over the doorway was a handpainted sign in black letters: "Melchor Ocampo School." My mother, familiar with the history of her country, named her school after a native son of Michoacán, a man who contributed greatly to nineteenth-century liberalism in Mexico. She wasn't anticlerical, but her secular education in Morelia, and my father's interest in politics and history, had made her sympathetic to progressive ideas from the mid-nineteenth-century conflicts between the Liberals and Conservatives. The front of the building was white, but the lower part of the wall was red with mud from the recent rain. A sizable window filled with a crisscrossed pattern of lead and small panes of glass interrupted the wall. One of the lower panes was broken, and mother had covered it with several pieces of heavy paper. Mama opened the door and we stepped in. Inside, part of the floor had been covered by tiles laid out in a diagonal pattern. The other section of the floor was packed dirt.

Part One

It was my job each morning to wet the floor down; after mopping the tile with a moist rag, I swept the dirt section lightly, directing the dust into the street. With both hands I carried a jug similar to Señora Gálvez's outside. Then I went back inside for my broom. I returned to the front of the school, closing the door behind me. The businesses on this street were less prosperous than those surrounding the plaza. Therefore, we did not have a drainage ditch to make the street more passable in the wet season and to provide a refuse for trash. I reached into the pot, cupping my hands to hold enough water to scatter over a small area. I eyed a rectangular section in front of our building and began to cover it with squares of water until I had completed the entire area like a patchwork quilt. Picking up the pot, and using the remainder of the water, I tried to wash the mud from the front wall. My efforts were not very successful. With the broom I imitated the sweeping motions of adults, starting at waist height and working my way down the wall.

"Pita, pita, pita." I heard the girl across the street call the hens for their morning meal. She lived in a small, run-down house between two businesses, separated from the street by a small yard and low natural wall of stones. I stopped to watch the hens and a cock scramble toward her feet as she tossed partial handfuls of the roughly ground corn to the soil. I waved and asked her if she was coming to school today. She nodded in assent.

Her family could not afford the regular fee, but my mother, reminded of her own past, allowed them to pay only what they could afford, so that their oldest child, Rosalia, might attend class.

The children arrived over a period of an hour since some of them came from a distance of five to six kilometers. When I had finished sweeping, I went inside where mother was outlining the day's lessons. She looked up from her work and,

24

seeing that I had finished my regular chores, gave me an additional job of wiping the slate.

I took the rag and stood on a small backless chair to wipe off the chalkboard. The long streaks of moisture quickly evaporated. When I had finished, I put the chair back into the corner, opened the door, and ran outside to play. Rosalia, who was latching a rickety gate of dead branches with a piece of twine, was turned partly away from me. She was my best friend. I still remember her features clearly. A small cotton dress fitted tightly around her slender frame. Perpetually barefoot, her feet were always covered by a thin coat of dust. Her face was round, with the soft, squeezable cheeks of a baby and dimples that made her seem to always be smiling. She wore two simple silver earrings. Her hair was black, braided like my mother's.

She skipped toward me, carrying a slate in one hand. She invited me to go to the stream. Leaving the slate on the sill of the window, we scurried off down the street.

Not very far down the lane there was a break in the walls. This small alley, bordered on both sides by walls intertwined with bouganvilla, led to a small arroyo covered with a variety of trees, which formed a canopy of green, filtered light. At the bottom of the arroyo ran a small stream winding around fallen trees and large stones washed into the valley by heavy rains.

I held Rosalia's hand as we descended awkwardly down a worn, slippery path, etched by miniature arroyos and gullies from the previous night's rainfall. I slipped halfway down, making two short skids in the mud. As soon as my bottom hit the mud I stopped. Remembering my clothes, I knew my mother would not be happy about me getting them dirty. Of course, that was a disadvantage of having your mother be your teacher. Rosalia helped me to my feet and tenderly brushed me off. I was embarrassed that I had fallen, while she had remained so steady. But she was slightly older than me, stronger and better coordinated. While she mothered me as a sister would a younger brother, I romanticized her as a girlfriend.

When we reached the water, I searched among the trunks for several large twigs. My search was short. I held up some sticks, showing her what I had found. Rosalia, who had found a smooth boulder on which to sit and dangle her feet in the shallow but turbid water, complimented me on my choices. Holding them out to her, I asked her to help me break them.

She took several from my fingers, slid one beneath the calloused heel of her small foot, and lifted the other end in her hand. "Crraack!" Bark fell off as she bent each twig across the top of her foot. One was too green and we could not break it. I took one and tossed it into the water, watching it disappear and reappear in our miniature river.

"Where do you think they go, Toño?" she asked.

"I don't know." I thought for a moment, then said, "I hope they go to Mexico."

"The big city?" she wondered aloud.

I nodded in the affirmative.

She asked me why. I told her I dreamed of visiting Mexico City, so I wanted my boats to visit it. My father had gone there and I too wanted to go. I suppose as a child I had not formed my reasons well. Somehow, I wanted to retrace my father's explorations. For someone like me from a small village in central Mexico, to ultimately visit Mexico City, the Paris of my culture, was truly an adventure of epic proportions. Those of us who succeeded in guiding Mexico's future had to have such an inquisitive spirit, regardless of the reason, to sustain our personal quests. Ultimately, the reason why I wanted to travel to Mexico City remained unimportant. That I wanted to go, however, was everything.

"My aunt says the city is a very bad place," she mused.

"Why is that?" I responded, surprised.

"I don't know. She says people are evil there. They have forgotten God."

I contemplated Rosalia's aunt's warning. I wondered if my friend actually believed what her aunt said. Today as I recall that conversation, I realize just how much she sounded like a character one would find in Agustín Yáñez's novels about rural Jalisco. Such religious cautions did not make much of an impact on me then as a child, or later as an adult. The mixed heritage of my mother's moderate religious beliefs and my father's secular Liberal beliefs, instilled in me a sense of independence even as a child. Like an early convert to Enlightenment thinking, I wanted evidence for everything. I readily distinguished between the admonishments of some adults versus others. Somehow, if exposed to different points of view, even children can develop a sense of cynicism about adult mythologies and explanations. My mother was never dogmatic about her religion, our upbringing, or her politics. If she didn't know the answer to something, she would always say so. One value she was dogmatic about, however, was her belief that a truth existed for every question; we only needed the correct book or source to find it. Thus, knowledge was her prejudice.

I tossed in another stick somewhat longer than the first, and I could still see it when it was nearly twenty feet downstream. I knew that my path would—better yet should—lead me from Purépuro. I had an unsatiable curiosity for the world beyond our home and village. I wanted to be part of that world, and also, I wanted to understand it. Rosalia couldn't completely understand those desires, but she was sympathetic. She was trustworthy. Without fear of betrayal, I could express all of my thoughts to her. She never criticized my wildest fancies. We talked for awhile, then suddenly remembering school, we decided we should return. I removed my sandals and we helped eath other up to the rim of the arroyo. As we walked back through the alley to our street, I told her how much fun I had had.

Six years later she was dead. The lively, beautiful face was stilled in the influenza epidemic that swept Mexico in deadly accompaniment to the martial violence of those years. Rosalia died without having seen a doctor or having slept on a bed. Fate was impartial—to both of us.

Part Two

Morelia:
A New Journey

1916 – 1919

5

Departure

Days varied little in Purépero. The simplicity of our lives had created some degree of stability; but when I reached twelve, this serenity ended when I entered secondary school in Morelia, the cultural and political capital of Michoacán. Because of my mother's profession, I had the opportunity to complete the four grades of primary education. The only secondary school in our region was located in Morelia. In fact, no secondary schools existed until 1925, and people fortunate enough to receive a primary education either stopped or joined a select few attending preparatory school.

During the 1910s, the revolutionary governments in Michoacán encouraged the expansion of preparatory education, providing some scholarships to promising students from rural villages. My mother's uncle, who was a friend of Governor Elizondo, put my name forth as a candidate for one of these scholarships. At the end of 1916, I received assistance to attend the Colegio Primitivo y Nacional de San Nicolás de Hidalgo in Morelia. Unlike the reactions of most parents of peasant background, my mother enthusiastically encouraged me to accept the scholarship since she saw education as the key to the future for me and my sister.

Soon I began to make preparations for my first trip outside the village. In reality my preparations were more emotional than practical since I had little to take with me. On my last evening at home, mother and grandmother held a small fiesta to celebrate my imminent departure. Some of our more musical townsmen, who played during celebrations of national holidays such as the Cinco de Mayo, played lively music to entertain us. All of my childhood friends were there, including my beloved Rosalia, and we danced together under the watchful eyes of the adults. A local group played a popular love song, "Hay un Ser."

> There's someone who's the god of my life
> Whose name softens my heart;
> When asleep, he appears in my dreams,
> When awake, he kills me with pain.
>
> I love him with love of fire
> The passion in my heart is consuming.
> And never shall I love the hope
> That we two shall meet again.*

My dreamlike trance was broken when Señor Romero shouted for the music to cease.

"Friends, friends, I have an announcement to make. Antonio is a true son of our village. Many of us knew his father, a fine man. Much has happened to us these past years, but this boy has had a bit of good fortune. He will represent the sons and daughters of Purépero in Morelia. Because he goes

*Frances Toor, *A Treasury of Mexican Folkways* (New York: Crown Publishers, 1947), p. 441.

as a native son and not just as Antonio Gutiérrez, we want him to go with pride."

He paused, handing me a tooled suitcase with sturdy hand-sewn seams and my initials, AGE, carved below the grips. I was speechless at the sight of this gift. He prodded me to look inside. Meanwhile, everyone crowded around. I opened the suitcase, and inside, neatly folded, was a black, wool suit, a white shirt with a stiff round collar, and some high-top leather shoes, none of which I had ever before owned. My friends gasped before I did. Señor Romero explained that my father's friends had purchased the gifts. Numb with surprise, I mumbled my thanks to them.

Children and adults alike cheered and clapped, and the music started up again. So ended my last night in Purépero.

The next morning grandmother woke me before the sun came up. I rose early to take Señor Romero's cart to Morelia, just as my father had done many years before me. As I got dressed, the stale smell of tamales and pulque, which still pervaded our rooms, stung my nose.

While putting on my clothes, I felt for the first time a weakening of will to leave. Plainly, I was scared. Since Rosalia had gone home, I confessed my fear to my grandmother. In her simple but thoughtful way, she had an answer. After these many years, I still remember her advice.

"Of course, child. That's only natural. This is a great journey that you take."

I wanted to know if I would fail.

"No Toño, you will succeed if you judge people with care," she assured me. "People can help you or hurt you. Learn to trust. But learn who to trust. Be friendly like the dog, but careful like the fox."

I told my grandmother I would try to follow her advice. In fact, I promised, I would remember everything she had ever told me.

Part Two

"Ha! You flatter your old grandmother," she said with a low chuckle. "I love you like a son."

While I finished dressing in my new clothes, grandmother made breakfast and wrapped some extra tortillas for my trip. Mother got up, leaving Camila asleep on the bed they shared.

She glanced at me in my new outfit, suggesting I looked quite ready for the trip. The suit fitted fairly well, but the sleeves were too short and my arms felt restrained in such clothes. The shoes, however, felt the strangest of all. I did not have socks, the stiff leather rubbed the tops of my toes, and my ankle bones felt trapped. She must have noticed my awkward grimace as I shuffled my feet hesitantly across the floor.

"You will get used to them son," she assured me, patting my shoulder. "You will grow into them like a new pair of *huaraches*."

I was still chewing my breakfast when the wagon stopped in front of our door. Mother greeted the driver and called to me. I hugged and kissed her. I climbed aboard the wagon laden with goods from local merchants who paid Señor Romero to take them to Morelia and the *municipios* of Carapan or Quiroga, both of which we would pass through on our way to the capital. Mother handed me my precious new suitcase. We said our goodbyes.

Her last words as we departed were, "Don't forget to write. Jorge can bring a letter back on his monthly trip."

She didn't actually cry, but her hand covered her mouth and nose, as though she were shielding the inevitable from my eyes. Even in her personal sadness she remained supportive, giving me the encouragement I desperately needed to carry out this decision.

Jorge had saved a place behind the seat, and I let my bag slide into it. He flicked a small whip over the backs of the two mules and the wagon lurched forward. I waved to my mother and grandmother until we rounded the corner heading back to

34

the main street. Turning onto the road that led out of the village, I glanced back at the distant plaza and the alamo trees where I had spent many happy hours. Jorge, settling into the worn, uneven wooden seat, looked beyond the heads of the mules as he spoke.

"Well *joven*," he said drily, "we are on our way to the city."

"Yes, the city. What is it like?"

Jorge sighed. "You will see Antonio, it's a long trip."

6

Morelia

The trip took several days, but to me it seemed short. Each turn in the road brought a new sight. I saw several high peaks, part of the volcanic chain that surrounds this region. In some places the road was only a track, so our pace was quite slow. We crossed several deep arroyos much wider than those near my village. On the morning of the fourth day we entered the city.

The architecture was striking. Built during the colonial period, the city retained a strong Spanish flavor. Much of the original aqueduct, like those I studied in ancient history, stood intact. The buildings were fronted with spacious arcades which duplicated the arches of the aqueduct. A mysterious sense of the past drew over me as Jorge guided the wagon through streets choked with carts and beasts of burden carrying wares to and from the commercial section. The noise from the squeaking wheels and animals, and human shouts sharply contrasted with the quiet of Purépero.

We passed within a block of the central plaza. I could see the Palacio de Gobierno, a building that would attract much of my attention in the months to come. Accustomed to Purépero's pine torches blackening posts around the square, I was fascinated that Morelia had gas lamps fastened to ornate, wrought-iron frames. I lost sight of the plaza as we crossed the street and ambled into an alley. Even through the eyes of a child, I knew my village had only the rudiments of city life, no municipal services, no lights, sewage, paved streets, sidewalks, or other amenities we expect fair-sized cities to have. Many villages similar to ours did not even have a priest, a school, or a teacher. The political leadership was often informal and not overtly visible. Essentially, we were a collection of people who lived in close proximity to each other but in many respects remained independent. Many years later, while reading histories of nineteenth- and early twentieth-century North America, I was struck not only by the independence of the pioneers and farmers who resembled our own forebearers, but also by their willingness to form tight-knit communities that made sacrifices for the good of the town rather than primarily for the good of the family. We have had our civic-minded citizens, too, but the theme they represent seems less common to Mexico.

Jorge was unperturbed by the continual, fast-paced motion of visitors and inhabitants. He easily guided the mules to a pale yellow building fronted by a dock built of heavy planking. The wagon seat remained slightly above the floor level of the planking. He pulled back on the reins, stopping the cart as he stepped over me to the dock. He tied the reins in a half hitch around a pole supporting the roof.

He instructed me to jump out and stretch my legs while he asked the owner the location of my school. Jorge stepped to the windowless back of the building and pulled down a large leather loop hanging through a pear-shaped hole in the right side of two heavy, unpainted doors. He disappeared inside.

I walked around the dock, then leaned up against the adobe wall. Looking down at my new shoes I noticed a heavy coat of dust covering the tongue and laces, and even more of the fine, sandy powder clinging to my suit. I looked like someone who had worked in the storeroom of a Dos Caras talcum factory. I slapped the sides of my pants with the palms of my hands and kicked the toes of my shoes into the floor of the dock. Only the top layer came off.

The door opened and Jorge led a young boy, about my age, blinking into the sunlight. He introduced me to Ramón. Ramón smiled shyly and nodded, repeating my greeting.

Jorge continued, explaining that Don Emiliano, the owner, would permit Ramón to accompany me to the school. I thanked Jorge for his help and asked Ramón to wait while I picked up my belongings. I pulled the suitcase and my coat from the wagon. Feeling a little homesick, I asked Jorge to tell my mother I had arrived safely. He assured me he would return in about six weeks. If I had a message or letter, I could leave it with Don Emiliano.

Ramón, barefoot, leaped from the dock. I set the bag on the edge, and with one hand holding on for support, I too jumped to the ground. Ramón, in a natural manner, lifted the bag down from the dock and began to carry it. Impressed by my dress and destination, he assumed we were from different classes. As a youngster from a humble family, I had not yet learned about the culture of class interactions. It took me many years before I felt at ease in a middle-class, urban environment. But at that moment, my first experience of being treated as someone above my social origins, I couldn't accept the prerequisites of my new identity.

"No, no, you don't have to carry it. I will," I insisted, taking the bag from his hand. He smiled again, said thanks, and we trudged off down the alley. I asked if he attended the Colegio. He said no, that he was a student at the Escuela Comercial of Padre Ojeda, on the corner of the Jardín de Capuchinas, where he was enrolled in a stenography course.

I asked him what he did at Don Emiliano's store. He explained that he worked as an accountant's assistant in order to pay for his schooling. He told me I was very lucky to be attending the Colegio, because it was a beautiful place with many fine professors. I agreed with him wholeheartedly, noting how fortunate I was to have received a government scholarship.

We turned again and walked down a cobblestone street. Conversing with Ramón, I did not pay much attention to the directions we took.

"This is the Parque Juárez," he announced, as we turned another corner and walked parallel to it. I had never seen anything like it. There was a lake, which I later learned rented small boats. Beautiful flowers and colorful foliage grew throughout the park. I remarked upon the beauty of the place.

I told Ramón that I hoped we could be friends. He agreed enthusiastically, and we discussed many other things. I wanted to know if he knew any other students at the Colegio.

"I have several good friends," he replied. "We have a group which serenades in the evenings to earn extra money. It is nothing too serious, but we have a good time, we get to sing songs from our regions, and all of us need the money. I'll introduce you to them." I told him that would be helpful and asked when he would complete his studies.

"Oh," he paused, "I think in another year, then I will attend the new normal school."

He told me his goal was to be a teacher. But of more immediate concern to me at that time was where he lived. I was hoping that he might live nearby. He explained to me that he lived with other students at the Casa de Estudiantes, a boarding house run by Mrs. Abigail Nicolás. According to Ramón, some of the students residing there went to my institution. Returning my question, he asked where I would live. I replied, shrugging my shoulders, that I wasn't sure—I only knew that it was somewhere at the Colegio.

Hearing Ramón's story, I felt all the more grateful for my good fortune. For Mexicans like me, only the luckiest of us would receive a preparatory and professional education. For another group, often from poorer circumstances and less fortunate, a primary or secondary teaching career would be their only chance for upward mobility. Only a few Mexicans, with or without scholarships, could afford the luxury of the kind of education I would receive at the Colegio. For boys like Ramón who had no additional help but a strong desire for knowledge, normal school was the shortest and most economical path to a better life. Many revolutionaries had themselves been schoolteachers, among them Plutarco Elías Calles.

We approached a high wall bordering the street, walking along it for some time before arriving at the gate to the Colegio. Ramón opened it, and after peering around the deserted courtyard, called out several times for the watchman. Silence. Then, behind the corner of one of the buildings, I heard the scraping sound of *huaraches* sliding across the tiles.

An older man, hatless, with dirty white trousers and a torn shirt, approached us and greeted Ramón. When he spoke, I noticed several front teeth missing.

I was introduced to Gregorio, who asked if I would be staying at the Colegio. He said that several other students had arrived, who, like me, were on scholarships. After saying goodbye to Ramón, Gregorio explained that I would be staying in a room with these students over the Escuela de Artes y Oficios. He explained that tomorrow I would visit Professor Oviedo, the director. I thanked him for his help. A well-fed cat edged softly in between us, and I trailed Don Gregorio up the stairs to my new home.

7

Colegio
de
San Nicolás

After taking me to the small dorm, Gregorio left. The room
was empty except for some sparse furnishings. Half a dozen
beds were lined up along one wall. These were handmade,
squat but sturdy, and although they had no springs, each contained a thin mat that served as a matress. My mother slept in a
bed, but this was the first time I had one of my own. Between
each bed was a small, scarred wooden table. In front of the
tables stood square, unattractive chairs matching the tables.

Choosing one of the beds not in use, I laid my suitcase down
on its side and sat on the edge. Exhaustion quickly overtook me
after this day of tense excitement and expectations. I opened
my suitcase and unpacked my belongings, placing them in
a narrow, elongated chest at the foot of my bed. After removing my shoes and laying my clothes out on top of the chest, I
crept under the dull-striped, rough woolen blanket, and fell
asleep.

The next morning I was awakened by the noise of voices
and people moving about. A tall, thin boy with slightly protruding ears and curly hair combed straight back was the first

to notice my sleepy-eyed attempt at waking up.

He shouted, "Look, muchachos, our new companion is alive!"

I introduced myself and a chorus of voices returned the greeting. The tall boy began a series of introductions. His name was Germán Torres. Beside him, only half-dressed, was a boy with strong Indian features—sunken, melancholic eyes and thick, black hair, closely cropped on the sides and top. His name was Silvestre Vázquez, whom I later learned to call El Indio. On the far side of the bed stood a boy of medium stature, with wide but rounded shoulders, and a hair line that was already receding. He introduced himself as Leopoldo Vela. The group called him El Médico.

Germán asked about my trip. He suggested that after we dressed and ate, he would take me to see Professor Oviedo. We had a quick breakfast on the street, purchasing fruits and other items from street-side vendors at a nearby plaza. After our meal, Germán accompanied me to the director's office. We entered an outer vestibule, where we encountered the director's secretary, Señor Carbajal, seated behind a small desk. After a brief introduction, the secretary motioned us to sit down.

Señor Carbajal knocked and quickly entered the inner office. Shortly, the door opened and he motioned for me to enter. Holding the door open, he followed me into the room toward a spacious, imposing desk directly opposite the doorway. The secretary introduced me to the director.

Professor Oviedo greeted me. He was the first formally attired gentleman I had ever met. He was dressed in a dark suit with wide lapels, his coat buttoned toward the top, as was the custom of his generation. He wore a stiff, white shirt with a curved collar that hung out over the coat and a large cravat tied beneath it. A small, square-linked, gold chain hung beneath the opening of his coat.

44

Part Two

After some polite formalities, he explained the obligations of a scholarship student.

"Each of your companions has a task at the Colegio. Your job will be to assist the regular staff in the library." Looking me straight in the eye, he continued, "You are fortunate, Antonio, because this position will not only help to finance your necessities here but will also provide you with a useful education. Take advantage of it to broaden your knowledge of Mexico and the world."

I assured him I would take full advantage of these opportunities.

"Good. You will receive a small, monthly stipend from Señor Carbajal. This sum will cover your expenses here. Some of the students take on extra jobs outside the school to provide themselves with extra spending money. However," he cautioned, "you only should take on such responsibilities gradually until you become more familiar with the obligations you already are committed to."

I thanked him for the advice and his explanation of my responsibilities. He told me to visit him any time I had questions or needed assistance. School did not start until the following week. That evening Ramón came as promised, and I went out with him and his companions. Some of them were from Morelia and attended the Colegio. I befriended several of them, but Ramón was to become my closest companion. After we had eaten, the other boys decided to play their instruments in the Parque Juárez in the hope of earning some money from passers-by.

Ramón asked if I would like to accompany their group. When I assented, he wanted to know if I played an instrument, and suggested that I might like to join his group "Las Espuelas" (The Spurs). I told him I would like to join, but that I did not play an instrument, although I knew many Tarascan songs. Ramón didn't think that my inability to play a musical instrument was significant. He said I could probably add some different songs to those they already knew and that a strong voice was equally needed.

The others agreed. That evening we played many revolutionary songs. I remember, most clearly, that our first song was the popular but sad "Adelita":

> At the top of a steep hill
> a regiment was encamped,
> with a girl who bravely followed it
> and who was deeply in love with the Sergeant.

> Popular among the men was Adelita,
> the woman whom the Sergeant idolized,
> and who in addition to being brave was pretty,
> so that even the Colonel respected her.

> And he who loved her so much was heard to say:
> If Adelita were to go with another,
> I should follow her over land and sea;
> if by sea in a warship,
> if on land in a military train.

> And if Adelita wishes to be my sweetheart,
> and if Adelita were to be my wife,
> I should buy her a dress of silk
> and take her to dance in the barracks.

> And after the cruel battle was over
> and the troops returned to camp,
> through the voice of a woman crying,
> a prayer was heard throughout the camp.

> And on hearing her the Sergeant,
> fearful of losing his beloved forever,

hiding his pain under a mask,
sang to his beloved thus:

And he who was dying was heard to say:
If I should die on the field of battle,
and if my remains are to be buried,
Adelita, for God's sake, I beg you
cry for me with your eyes.

We played and sang until 11:00 P.M., taking donations from anyone who offered them. At the end of the evening, we had earned nearly a peso, which we divided, despite my protests, into five equal parts.

"When school begins, Toño, we play regularly, except during vacations, on Friday, Saturday, and Sunday evenings," explained Ramón. "You are welcome to join us." I thanked Ramón and told him I would like to continue to participate. Then remembering the director's advice, I hastily added that I would sing with them unless my schoolwork and job took up too much time.

We walked together back toward their boarding house, and Ramón left the others so that he could accompany me to the Colegio. He asked me about my classes. I had talked with the other students in my dorm, two of whom were in their second year. My first year would be fixed, with no elective courses. It included Latin, Spanish, Spanish Literature, Mathematics, Science, and History.

Ramón listened carefully to my description. He thought that I was very fortunate to take mathematics. The subject fascinated him, but his business school did not offer any mathematics courses beyond basic accounting.

I asked why he was so interested in math. His answer was simple. "Because I'd like to be an engineer, Toño, to build

48

great bridges and good roads to make my village and your village a more important part of Mexico. It's a dream I have."

"But I thought you wanted to be a teacher," I countered.

"That's my immediate goal, and one which is most possible for me. But to be an engineer, that's my real dream."

The fulfillment of Ramón's dream would have many positive results for Mexico. When you live in the small world of a Mexican village, it is difficult to comprehend the importance of building roads. For peasants, the most obvious benefit would be transportation to and from the village. Without a doubt, roads, which were built everywhere by members of my generation, were essential to our economic development. But transportation of goods and resources to and from rural areas was only one among many goals. Perhaps the most important long-term impact of the dream which Ramón visualized was the influx of ideas. I'm convinced that we have progressed as a nation because of the communication of knowledge. Indeed, there are still many parts of our country that are not well connected to the city, especially in the South and the mountainous parts of the West. But the radio, and in some cases television, can be found in the most remote and isolated regions of Mexico. Our people move to the cities in droves seeking work and a chance, like Ramón and I had, to alter their lives.

He asked me about my own goals. I told him, "I'm still unsure. There is so much to know. For now, I'm excited by all of my subjects. Perhaps I'll be a teacher. I'm very interested in our history. I want to know more about the Revolution and about the men who have led it."

Ramón told me that he had a friend who worked with General Múgica's group. He suggested that I talk to him about the Revolution. I pleaded with Ramón to introduce me to his friend. He promised that if I would visit him at the store the

49

next morning, he would try to arrange a meeting. I agreed to meet him. I also promised to bring some mathematics and engineering books from our library.

Our long walk ended quickly after such an earnest conversation. We approached the familiar wall again and parted.

8

Andrés

The next morning was one of those unusually sunny, cloud-less, days of early summer. I skipped breakfast after sleeping late, and started walking to the store where Ramón worked. On my way I encountered an old fruit vendor, hatless, with a large red bandanna tied over his head selling his wares on a street corner. His oranges looked delicious. Tempted, I stopped to buy one for breakfast. Fastened to his cart, with wire and manila twine, was a small, metal machine. When I selected an orange he asked me if I would like it peeled. I said yes, and he put the orange between two steel prongs. Then he turned a small crank. As he did so the orange rotated over a small blade and a thin ribbon of peel snaked slowly from the fruit. I was amazed. In less than a minute the fruit was shaved clean.

Eating my orange, I continued down the street. I asked directions twice before finding the store. Inside, I inquired for Ramón. He came out of a room screened off from the rest of the store and asked me to wait.

I went out the door and looked around. To the left across from the storefront stood a low adobe wall, about two feet high. It was shaded by several bottlebrush trees whose scaly bark and bright carmine flowers lay scattered on top of and below the wall. I eyed the shade and walked across the street. Reaching the far side I crushed a number of the symmetrical, jarlike pods which had fallen to the ground beneath my feet. I dusted off a place on the wall and lay down along the top, propping my head up with the palm of my hand. It was a perfect position from which to watch the stream of people. Before long, a plump middle-aged woman passed in front of me surrounded by a dozen or so turkeys, one of which she kept leashed to her by means of a ragged piece of rope around its neck. She held the rope in her left hand, and with her right, she occasionally tapped and poked at a straying animal with a small, bare sapling. She cackled in a low voice, communicating to her charges in a tone similar to their constant gobbling. She shuffled along, setting the pace for their march, most probably, to market.

After watching several other interesting people, I spotted Ramón coming through the doorway. I waved, simultaneously swiveling my hips to get up. We met half way across the street.

"My friend, Andrés, the person I told you about last night, teaches mornings at my school. If we hurry, we can catch him finishing his last class, and I will introduce you to him," said Ramón.

We walked hurriedly, conversing as we went. Ramón began describing his friend.

"Andrés is an interesting person. We first got to know each other because of our musical interests. His father is related to my landlady, so he lives in our guest house. He started out as a music student, largely because of family pressures. His father had been a successful musician as well as a practicing pharmacist. However, like you, he was intrigued with the subjects offered in the preparatory program at the Colegio. He switched programs without telling his parents. When his father found out nearly a year later, he cut off all funds, angered because he believes such an education is worthless. Andrés did not have enough money to continue so he taught primary school for a short while until he was able to secure a part-time position at the Escuela Comercial. His compadre, who is a member of Múgica's political faction, introduced him to the general. He has been working in support of Múgica for governor of Michoacán. Andrés is very radical and anti-Catholic in his views. He has met many other politicians and military men."

We approached a two-story building. I could read the name in large blue letters, indicating a business school. In front stood a number of boys and girls my age, who by their dress were from poor families. They were talking, joking, or reading their books.

We picked our way through the milling students into the main sala. Ramón asked a slender, smiling girl if his friend had left. She shook her head. We proceeded to one of the small classrooms. There, we encountered a stocky young man with long legs and a short waist. His brown hair was combed to the side and a large clump hung over his forehead in an arc to the top of his ear. He wore gold frame glasses, his eyes magnified by their thick, completely round lenses. They were slightly too narrow across his brow, contributing to the exaggerated size of his cheeks. A short, thick scar was easily visible on his face, extending from the tip of his eyebrow to just short of the hairline. He was explaining the roots of a certain Spanish phrase to two students. As he talked he emphasized his points by clenching his left hand and thrusting his right hand in a downward motion with the palm up and fingers closed together. This he did constantly with the rhythm of his speech. We waited until the students were satisfied with the explanation and had left the podium.

Catching sight of Ramón, he greeted him warmly with an

embrace. Ramón introduced me as a student at the Colegio, interested in Mexican history, especially the Revolution. He insisted that Andrés would enjoy discussing his experiences and readings with me.

Andrés agreed that he would be pleased to speak with me, and invited us both to have coffee. Ramón had to return to work, but I happily accepted the invitation. We chatted on our way out, and Ramón left for the store. Andrés took me to a small café frequented by students and professors from several of the local schools. He spoke to many people before sitting down at a small table and ordering each of us a cup of coffee. Leaning back in his chair he pulled a pack of cigarettes from his vest pocket, smoothly extracting one and tapping it on the flat side of the package. Striking a match swiftly against the bottom of the table he lit the cigarette, puffing furiously as we talked. We discussed our respective backgrounds, and then more intellectual topics.

"Do you know much about the contemporary affairs of Mexico, Antonio?"

"Not really," I said, shaking my head. "I have received only limited information about such subjects in Purépero. We really couldn't afford a newspaper."

"Much has happened at the Convention of Querétaro, held not too far from Mexico City," he explained. "Revolutionaries of all viewpoints joined there to write out a document replacing the old liberal Constitution of 1857. They have made some important changes, producing new articles concerning the role of the Catholic Church, the ownership of land, the rights of labor, and many other social and political propositions. Do you know about this convention?"

I told him I had heard vague rumors from my older friends and from my compadre. Later I would learn the provisions of the Constitution of 1917, as any school child does today, in detail. But for me, and for my generation, the Constitution itself was more important than the content of its controversial articles, many of which have been altered and amended as the years passed. For me the Constitution served as an essential guidepost of political life. That is, during the years I grew to adulthood the concept of a constitution as a reflection of our social and political goals, a document with supreme legitimacy among the Mexican people, also passed from creation to maturity. My friends call it constitutionalism. Constitutionalism is like an organic body, it grows and emerges in a society. You can create a document of laws, but it has little meaning unless the citizens and officeholders inherently respect it. Of course, I am not foolish enough to suggest that in our political system we obey all the rules set down in writing but, as the concept evolves, evasion becomes increasingly difficult. But in my adolescent years, I still had much to learn and was eager to do so with Andrés.

"Well then, we'll have to tutor you in recent political events. You said you'll be working in the library?"

Since I was employed there, he advised me to read the Mexico City paper each day, and to read several books on the social problems of Mexico. He recommended them as excellent criticisms of what he described as the foul deeds of the Díaz dictatorship. Andrés's ideas were decidedly well formed. By contrast my views lacked a basis in knowledge and were vague. Informed opinions would come later. After plying me with advice he asked if I had some interest in political affairs.

I assured him that I was interested in politics. Andrés decided I was worth recruiting, and explained, "As Ramón probably told you I am a supporter of General Múgica, a great revolutionary of national fame. I am now involved in his campaign to win the governorship of Michoacán. He is campaigning against Ingeniero Pascual Ortiz Rubio, another revolutionary, but a moderate and a man of mediocre talents. We are always in need of workers to publicize the merits of the General to the people of Michoacán. Time is running short and the election will be held soon. If you have time why don't you come with me and learn first-hand about some of the political issues?"

I thanked him for the invitation, and told him I would try to participate. We discussed politics for well over an hour. During this time Andrés consumed three cups of coffee and twice as many cigarettes, a habit he retained throughout his life. His invitation to involve myself in a political campaign was to be the first of many during the next decade.

9

The Election

The following Monday I began classes. After several weeks, despite my interest in all of the subjects, I began to favor the social science and literature courses. My job at the library, while taking away scarce time from my studies and my limited social life, did, as Professor Oviedo predicted, open up many doors to greater knowledge. Following Andrés's suggestion I began to read *El País*, a major Mexico City paper. Later, I read the *Revista de Revistas*, a literary periodical devoted to contemporary writing by Mexican intellectuals. After settling into a fairly regular routine and adjusting to dormitory life, I began to participate each Friday evening in the serenade group. On Sunday mornings, Ramón and I took long exploratory walks through Morelia and into the surrounding countryside.

The routine of school, however, was not the only activity filling the months, which passed by so quickly. Finding more questions than answers in my readings on recent Mexican history, I committed myself to helping Andrés in the gubernatorial campaign and devoted extra time on Saturdays to the campaign. Andrés became the assistant to the private secre-

tary of General Múgica. As his helper, I had access to much of
the correspondence between the General and his revolutionary friends throughout Mexico. This experience increased my
contact with both young and old political activists attracted
to the campaign because of the romantic appeal of the new
revolutionary ideology and because of the opportunities for
sinecures if our candidate won. Despite my naïveté, I learned
several lessons from this experience.

Near the conclusion of the campaign, I traveled overnight
with Andrés to a small town about a day's ride from Morelia.
This community's support was hotly pursued by both groups,
and the mayor was known to favor Ortiz Rubio. In addition to
the fact that Múgica had several supporters among the more
prominent revolutionaries in the village, he hoped to use his
personal appearance to gain popular support. There were ap-
proximately a dozen persons in our group. The trip to the village was uneventful, but as soon as we reached the outskirts
of the village we were approached by a lone horseman. Dressed
like a townsman, he greeted several members of the General's
immediate retinue familiarly. We reined in our horses and
stretched in the saddles as we waited for further instructions.
The word was passed that the horseman had brought news of
possible harassment and violence in the village square. The
general said we would continue, but cautiously.

When I asked who was responsible for such behavior,
Andrés replied "It's difficult to know, Toño. There could be
several sources. Sometimes local politicians, in the hope of
pleasing their superiors, attempt to create a poor showing for
the opposition candidate by scaring him off or preventing him
from speaking. They expect to be rewarded accordingly."

I asked if this practice was common elsewhere in Mexico.

"Those who are in the strongest position often use this
method. But in this case those responsible, although probably
not in this village, might include the president himself, or his

closest subordinates." Andrés explained further that, "General Múgica has many enemies, in part because of his well-known political stance at the Constitutional Convention. Furthermore, Carranza, like other presidents before him, is attempting to put many of his supporters in power as governors because these men can help sustain his government and his views. To achieve this end, his Minister of Government often intervenes in support of just such a candidate. We, as you have already learned, are not the favored group in this election."

Not yet willing to accept defeat, I argued, "But in the copy of the new Constitution you gave to me, I thought two of the goals were effective suffrage and freedom of the *municipio* from federal intervention?"

Andrés laughed, "True, my young friend, but, to use your words, it is only a newly promulgated goal, not yet an achievement."

"Don't you agree, Andrés, that all candidates would benefit from the application of these goals?"

He admitted that in most cases my point would hold true. Encouraged by his agreement, I then asked why he thought people continued the abuses of the Porfiriato.

He paused for several moments before answering. "There's no simple explanation, Toño. I believe that many Mexicans of today are imitating the Mexicans of yesterday. Díaz was a terrible Mexican. But one of his political legacies, contributing to the poverty of our country, was his ability to retain office. He did so by controlling those who got the public offices and the private concessions. I think that by the end of his regime, many young people with political interests were more concerned with their lack of access to political positions than with the means of achieving them. We Mexicans hold on to our customs politically as well as socially. Despite our Revolution, and despite our changed attitudes, many men who want to implement changes believe the old political practices are the

Part Two

most reliable means of doing so. Therefore, local leaders continue to support regional leaders or the President in hopes of generous rewards and maintenance in office."

I grabbed the pommel of the saddle as we moved through a rocky and uneven section of the road. Reflecting on the last part of his explanation I asked why so many men called themselves revolutionaries if they compromised their positions by not supporting all of the principles of the Constitution?

He smiled. "You are very young, yet. You will learn that for most of us, life, as well as politics, is a compromise."

Not ready to capitulate, I insisted that he had not compromised his beliefs.

Laughing again, he tolerantly replied, "Your praise is appreciated. I don't really know, I like to think I haven't, and I hope not. But perhaps my sacrifices are still small enough to make compromise unnecessary. I believe I am a man of firm principles. But, who knows? General Obregón says no man can resist a cannon ball of fifty thousand pesos."

Our horses' footsteps echoed below the planking of the small bridge we crossed as we approached the village. I continued to think about what Andrés had said, but I let the conversation lapse as I sensed growing tension. We could see the village, and the houses stood closer together as we drew near the plaza. After several minutes of riding in silence we emerged into the open ground surrounding the plaza, unexpectedly encountering a small crowd of vociferous supporters, shouting and waving as they caught sight of their candidate. Still on horseback we mingled with the crowd, following the General toward a small cafe. Dismounting, we gave our reins to some young boys from the crowd, who took the horses across the plaza to be watered. A group of us sat down at some tables in a small outer dining area. Andrés ordered beer and I purchased a tasty white drink of water and ground rice. I questioned Andrés about the possibility of trouble.

Morelia, 1916–1919

"It's difficult to tell," he said, shrugging. "The General will be speaking in two hours. Perhaps they will agitate then."

We relaxed for half an hour, as large numbers of peasants and townspeople began gathering in the square. Our supporters had built a small platform with a short podium between two trees on the edge of the plaza. Andrés excused himself briefly to talk to his superior. He returned after several minutes, explaining that we should sit in the rows of chairs near the speaker's stand since some of the local *políticos* had arranged for entertainment in honor of General Múgica. We watched a striking performance of a *canacuas*, a local dance. Several men with stringed instruments, inluding a harp, formed a cluster behind the General, who was seated at a small table. Then, the crowd opened up and five or six beautifully dressed mestizas in long skirts with brightly embroidered blouses, stepped toward the center. Each wore a rebozo crossed like a bandolier. After reaching the open area they lifted bowls filled with fruit, flowers, and toys, and placed them on their heads, creating two files on either side of the General. They sang several songs, including one of my Tarascan favorites "La Flor de Canela." Of the dances, the most striking was the dance of the knot, in which a young man joined the maidens and, with one of them, tied a knot in a scarf with their feet.

After the entertainment, several local *políticos* made some introductory speeches, praising our leader and immodestly adding some laudatory comments about themselves, including exaggerations about their relationships to General Múgica. By now the crowd had grown large and restless. Toward the rear I noticed a scuffle and, as the last local supporter began to speak, shouts and catcalls came from the crowd. The speaker could barely be heard above the din, and when one speaker stood up and courteously asked for quiet, he was greeted by a barrage of overripe fruit; one piece struck the General on the shoulder. This sparked a reaction from the pro-Múgica sup-

61

porters and fighting broke out. The peaceful assembly turned into a brawl with curses and screams everywhere. Suddenly a shot was fired.

The conflict escalated as people pushed and shoved to escape the fray. Andrés grabbed my coat sleeve and pulled me to the back of the stand. There, General Múgica, no coward in such situations, suggested that both for our health and the campaign it might be better to leave since he did not want this incident used as a pretext to prevent him or any members of his immediate group from making further appearances important to his cause. We retreated to our horses as more shots were fired. As we quickly mounted, I noticed Andrés had pulled a small pistol from beneath his coat and stuck it visibly in his waist, near the buckle.

Most of the revolutionaries and *políticos* carried pistols during these years. In the late 1910s and 1920s, Mexico evolved from an era of widespread violence, personal and otherwise, to the dominance of the law. But the changes took place slowly, and even leaders found it necessary, or believed it prudent, to be prepared to protect themselves. Their use of personal weapons only symbolized the tenuousness of law. Many of us would feel naked when we finally removed our pistols in the 1930s, but to see a weapon in the hands of my schoolteacher friend then greatly surprised me. Later, after we were safely back in Morelia, he told me he always carried it during campaigns to protect his life. Several years later, I would understand why.

Part Three

Mexico City:
Another Journey
1920–1932

10

The City

The staccato click, click, click changed to a flat, hollow clack, clack, clack as the train crossed each trestle and bridge en route to Mexico City. It was my first time on a train. The three of us, Germán Torres, Leopoldo Vela, and I had decided to go to Mexico City to study. General Múgica finally became governor in 1920. Soon after, having developed a distaste for lawyers in general, especially those graduating from the Colegio de San Nicolás, he closed down the law school, disrupting the tranquil academic environment of my first three years. Because of my past affiliation with Andrés, Múgica continued my scholarship funds along with those for several other students wanting to complete their professional studies in Mexico City or at the University of Guanajuato.

The second-class car contained two rows of wooden seats set on scuffed, cast-iron frames. We carried all of our books and belongings with us in an assortment of suitcases and boxes. For meals we relied on hot dishes and fruits sold by vendors who thrust their wares through the train's window at each stop. Since the cars had no sanitary facilities, frequent stops were a necessity. Even today I can recall the odors of sweating bodies and small livestock crammed into the seats and most of the aisles. These smells combined with that of animal defecation and the urine of small children who were unable to wait for the next stop. All matter of fruit peels and refuse were strewn across the floor. Afraid of chills and mysterious illnesses, which air drafts might bring, most of our fellow travellers left the windows closed in transit.

We were getting closer to Mexico City. Germán indicated that we had just stopped at Atlacomulco, which meant that Toluca was the next major station before the capital. The train began climbing. The wheels screeched and strained as we rounded a curve through the pine-covered mountain slopes. We all agreed that this would be the last uphill section before our descent into Mexico.

Leopoldo interrupted, wanting to know if our lodgings would be close to the National Palace.

Germán replied affirmatively, "I think they are close together since the guest rooms are not far from the Preparatory School, and it is a close walking distance from the Plaza." All of our questions would be answered in the morning.

Our nervous excitement had worn off by late afternoon. Combined with the monotonous vibrations and the warm sun streaming through the greasy, unwashed windows, we each lapsed into a state of half-sleep.

By dusk, we had left Toluca and started down the mountain range into a spacious, bowl-shaped valley. With a murmur of "pardon me" and "with your permission," I squirmed through the passive bodies of fat women, aging men, soldiers in tattered uniforms, and several Indian couples. I reached the end of the car and pushed open the door leading to a small platform connecting our car to the next. Keeping my balance, I edged toward the railing and grabbed hold of an upright pole. With the wind rushing through my hair, I let my face enjoy an entirely new experience—speed. I watched the heavy metal hitches as they rose and fell, like boats at anchor, first pushing and then tugging as each car shifted its weight. Then came a click and a sucking noise as a man emerged from the next car. His hat identified him as the conductor. He was dressed in a white shirt, somewhat yellowed with age, and an ill-fitting black suit, with short sleeves.

Knowingly, the conductor asked if it were my first trip on board a train. I readily admitted his suspicions were correct. Hoping that he had visited other parts of Mexico, I asked him about his own experiences.

"Well, I've travelled in many parts of the Rep. . . . " Weeeeeeh, the whistle broke in on his words. "Republic with the Constitutionalists. But you know, I never get tired of it. Each trip has its surprises. Sometimes they're pleasant, sometimes not. One thing you can count on, it's always different each time."

Curious, I asked where he had travelled?

"Oh, I spent most of my time in the north, carrying General Obregón's troops."

"Did you know him personally?"

"No, no," he laughed, "only well enough to greet him. But I have seen him many times."

I asked him what he thought of his government.

"It's too soon to tell. Times are difficult. Our economy is stagnant. The papers say it's a result of the great war in Europe. It is much more than that. We've been fighting a long time. The destruction, well, these eyes have seen a lot of death. People are tired of violence. It becomes a sickness, like a cold. You get it too often, you eventually get used to it. We need some stability. We must take care of our own affairs. But I tell you, I like Obregón. A man of great calm in a crisis. Mexico would do well to have a dozen two-armed politicians with as much courage as the one-armed general. I'm putting my cards on him these days."

I agreed with his observations, although it would have been difficult to disagree with him. In those days you didn't start talking politics with someone unless you had some prior inclination about their views. A man's preference started many an argument, and sometimes those altercations led to serious unpleasantries, even death. The conductor probably spoke frankly because of my youth. Otherwise, he would have never brought up the subject. He asked about my background, and I told him I was from Michoacán.

"Ah, Múgica is in control now, no?"

I explained that after many struggles he finally reached the governorship. I told him about my political activities in Michoacán, and my involvement in Múgica's first gubernatorial campaign. Learning of my interest in politics, he asked if I liked political speeches. I admitted that sometimes I did.

He offered me some friendly advice. "Look, my young friend, if you're going to Mexico City you should visit the Chamber of Deputies. You can hear speakers there. I heard this fellow, . . . ah, what is his name? Manrique, yes, Professor Manrique. What a speaker! He's extraordinary. Go if you have a chance. I went in September with a friend. This man will bring chills to your spine."

I thanked him for the suggestion. He asked if I was a student. I told him I was going to study in Mexico City with some friends. He was very pleased to hear that. For some reason he wanted to praise me. The words stuck in my mind these many years.

"Young man, I commend you for attending school. I didn't have the opportunity. I regret not obtaining a better education. I read a lot, but it's not the same. Mexico needs educated men. We are at a new age. We need people like you and your friends to help achieve the Revolution's goals. It's time to end the violence. Knowledge and culture will give us the key to our future. We have much to do. I envy you. Your generation will lead Mexico's progress."

I took what he said to heart. It was a personal message, but it was a message for my generation. It's strange that you can meet someone you never met before, listen to a few words of advice, and they goad you on to better things. That has happened at several crucial points in my life. I told him I had many dreams for my country and that all of us would work hard for a better Mexico. He patted me on the shoulder and said he had to leave. I never saw him again.

I remained a few minutes longer on the platform before entering the car and pushing my way back to my seat. Germán and Leopoldo awoke. We could now glimpse the lights from the distant city. The air chilled noticeably, and drops of water began to splash against the windows, which were soon covered by a heavy coat of vapor. The minutes raced by quickly, the engine slowed, stopping altogether at the central station. As people poured out of both ends of the car we grabbed our belongings and followed the shorter of two lines. Once inside the poorly lit building we walked for some distance. An old man sitting on the wheel hub of a horse-pulled cart negotiated with us for a ride. Water poured off the brim of his straw hat as he helped pile our worldly goods into the cart. Soaked, we huddled together as he drove us toward our new home, a guesthouse for students from Michoacán. We saw little in the rain-drenched night. After what seemed an interminable ride, the cart jerked to a halt in front of a two-story building with a heavy wooden door and barred windows. Germán paid the driver while I ran, heavily laden, for the shelter of the doorway. Finding a large knocker, I lifted it and banged loudly on the door. Wet, shaking with cold, I stood waiting for an answer.

11

Back to School

The sun found its way through thousands of gaps in the cheap, chintz curtains. I looked up at the bare bulb hanging from a ragged cord. The ceiling sagged in the center. It had been a week since my wet arrival.

I immediately took a liking to my landlady, Señorita Graf, a woman dispossessed of most of her wealth, except her home, after the Revolution. She rented several rooms out on the second floor. The house itself had been attractive at one time, but with the change of fortunes of the owner, its upkeep, like that of many other post-revolutionary homes, had been neglected.

The walls were nearly a foot thick. My bedroom, while cramped, had a window overlooking a rickety staircase leading to a commercial printing shop. Voices shouting orders mixed with the clank of machinery constantly emanated from the doorway. Still, it was pleasant to have the sunlight in the morning and, in the afternoon, a refreshing breeze. My furniture was part of the original decor of the house, including a carved Italian chair with a primitive, more recently constructed desk. My ensemble included a chest of drawers, the first I had

ever used. On top of the chest was a framed mirror reflecting
a faded oil of Mary and the Christ child hanging on the opposite wall. I shared a bathroom with the occupants of several
other rooms as well as my landlady's brother.

Señorita Graf was the daughter of a publisher whose paper
strongly supported Porfirio Díaz. With the downfall of Díaz,
the paper's readers repudiated its editorial line, and its circula-
tion declined precipitously. Soon thereafter, the senior Graf
was killed in an equestrian accident. The señorita received her
parents' house since she was the only family member who had
not married or been engaged in some profession. She received
no other income, converting her ownership of the house,
like many Porfiristas, into an income. She rented out rooms
and provided meals for boarders. A goodhearted person who
shared the views of her generation, she would regale me with
vivid descriptions of her education in Paris, the experiences of
a young woman growing up in Mexico City, and the recollections of some of the notables who visited her home while her
father was alive.

Social elites no longer frequented her house, but the señorita
had several friends, old maids like herself, who visited. One
in particular, Amalia, was much older and had grown up in
Mexico during the 1860s. Quick-witted and interested in all
facets of life, Amalia, who walked with a limp and a cane,
instilled in me an understanding of history I could not learn
through books. She remembered the French intervention, the
presidency of Benito Juárez (who once shook hands with her),
and the climb to power of Porfirio Díaz. My understanding of
Mexico's history expanded from our vociferous discussions,
and my perspective became broader and more accurate. She
made Mexico's past come alive.

I learned something else from these women. I came to understand the importance of historical perspective. Historical truth
is opaque. What we learn about history, as is true in all so-

74

cieties, is the victor's point of view. They write the textbooks that we all must read. But naturally there are two sides to every conflict. I'm not suggesting that I agreed with their interpretation, but these Mexicans taught me to appreciate the existence of another point of view. We cannot oppress what we have defeated or we shall be condemned to repeating our history.

My friends taught me something else, too. They taught me that the young can never understand the context of their time, because they view the present in isolation. We need to understand the realities of our past to appreciate the present. Our judgments are flawed, while older people have a basis for comparison. In Mexico today, as in the United States, we have turned to youth for the solutions to these problems. We should never denigrate our youth, but how can they understand the severity of our problems when most of them have lived in relative affluence?

Señorita Graf and Amalia became my touchstone with the past, but my classes at the National Preparatory School brought me into the present. What instructors! I enrolled in 1921, and became part of the class graduating in 1924. Leopoldo Vela, who also took a room in my house, enrolled in the pre-medical preparatory program. Many of our classes were the same, but I was in the first group, whose names went through *J*, and he was in the second. Like most of my companions, I enrolled in the pre-law program. The teachers were excellent and, although some were still sympathetic to the Porfiriato, the classes were small and the reading opened up other vistas. Even so, much of my learning occurred in the hallways of the various arcades in the inner courtyard of the school, where my companions and I had long discussions between and after classes. It was during just such a discussion that I became involved in another activity.

Adolfo, one of my new classmates in Latin, asked me about my previous political experiences in Michoacán. I described my involvement with Múgica's campaign. He explained that a group of friends were interested in starting a student newspaper. They were looking for someone like me, with actual political experience under my belt, to write a column on politics. He asked if I would be willing to join their venture.

I told him I was, but I wanted to know how he could afford to publish it.

"Oh, don't worry about that," he assured me, "Miguel Alemán, one of the organizers, is going to pay for the paper and printing out of his allowance. You do know him, don't you, he's the son of General Alemán, from Veracruz?"

I did not know General Alemán, nor did I have any money to contribute, but I hoped their efforts would be successful. Adolfo explained that they planned to have an organizational meeting later in the week, and he would notify me in advance. It seemed to me that a student version of the news would provide a valuable addition to our sources of information.

Later in the week we met and decided to call our paper *Eureka*. No one knew where we could have it printed, so I suggested the shop next door to my room. I was chosen to talk to the owner and to discuss the cost. This I did, and we agreed on an inexpensive charge for our publication.

As the political writer for *Eureka*, I covered numerous activities. Remembering the suggestion of the trainman, I attended a session of the Chamber of Deputies. He was right, the debates were sometimes electrifying. Of course this was not true in later years, but then, in the 1920s, when genuine legislative competition existed, things were different. I began to write columns on national issues, especially covering the debates over the agrarian reform program. However, my columns were not confined to subjects of national interest. On the campus, much was happening in the way of student elections. Some of our supporters ran as representatives to the student federation of the Federal District and to the national association. We gave strong support to those we favored. This experience increased my passion for political and social issues, which was rekindled in later periods of my life.

As I look back now I sometimes think we were both naïve and arrogant. We were naïve to think that education made us knowledgeable about our times and what Mexico needed. We were somewhat arrogant in that we thought our governors should pay heed to our criticisms. Our comments often turned out surprisingly accurate. But students tend to have a theoretical view of life. We learned a great deal about politics competing with each other for elective office, but this competition was in an artificial environment confined to the city and among our peers. The man on the street wasn't involved. We were much more sensitive about all Mexicans because of our own humble roots than the affluent technocrats of the present generation. The academic environment of our era surely was more real than campus life since, but that doesn't entirely excuse us.

What I didn't realize at the time, however, is how much political life since the 1940s would emulate that student political world. In one sense, it was comparable. If you think of the National Preparatory School, and subsequently the National University as a singular political arena in which most of Mexico's future political leaders three decades later could be found, it becomes analogous to our political life. We were being tested. Impressions were formed. Skills were developed. Friends would come back to each other time after time for help in public and private life.

For my generation there wasn't a Great War, as the North Americans shared, or the Revolution itself, to test our steel. But our childhood, growing up in difficult times; our adolescence, attending school when resources and facilities were scarce; and our student political involvement—these shared

77

experiences molded our sense of camaraderie. We never were
able, even half a century later, to shake off our past nor to
deny our loyalties to those who endured it with us.

My first year as a preparatory student, or *prepa* as we were
called, passed quickly. In addition to my courses, I was busy
learning outside the classroom as well. I first became interested in art during this period, and collecting became a life-
long pursuit. José Vasconcelos, who was minister of education,
supported several of our great twentieth-century painters.
They began doing frescoes on public buildings, including the
National Preparatory School. Looking at those murals, I reminded myself of my cultural heritage, a heritage I hoped not
to forget in the midst of my transition from a provincial capital
to the large metropolis of Mexico City.

Leopoldo took an equal interest in art. One day we had
quite an argument about the purpose of art, especially its in-
herent aesthetic quality versus its contribution to the social
edification of the ordinary person. Leopoldo thought the murals were a bit crude.

I admitted that perhaps from the traditional view of art his
assertion was true, but I believed they conveyed so much feeling. "Besides," I argued, "the muralists are developing their
own style, a style which draws strongly on emotion."

He wasn't convinced. "But Toño, that isn't sufficient to be
called art. Art should have a certain beauty, or better yet, a
certain elegance. . . ."

I couldn't argue against that, but I wanted to know for whom
was this elegance. To emphasize my point, I applied my ideas
to him personally. "As a doctor you want to serve the Mexican
people, not just a class. You need to convey your understanding of their problems in a language they can understand,
while at the same time, you must represent the knowledge of
your profession."

"I guess I'd have to go along with that," replied Leopoldo, still unconvinced. "But shouldn't art be done for art's sake? I mean, these works have too much political commentary. What's happened to the beauty of it all? Your analogy doesn't ring true. There is nothing artistic about medicine. It fills a physical need, not an emotional one, at least directly."

"I understand what you mean, but beauty can be combined with a social or political interpretation. Surely, art can have both."

Taking a different tack, *El Médico* tried to probe me on the possible audience. "But can the *peon* understand this work?"

"I'm not entirely sure," I hesitated, "I think so. Besides, it might help him have a better understanding of life. It could be thought of as a large picture book for adults instead of children. Because it's on the wall, you can't pass it by. And best of all, there are no covers to open or pages to turn."

"Yes, but what if our interested peasant misinterprets the meaning of these public displays. What if he doesn't understand the message?"

Annoyed, I told him he was being unfair. "First you say the murals are simplistic, now you say the average citizen won't understand them. They can't be both. There's so much to do. Mexicans need education, this might be a way to that. What I'm trying to suggest is that Vasconcelos, through the muralists, has found a way to reach these people. I'm convinced we have an obligation to try any approach possible. Art is just one possibility. Think about it, Leopoldo. We could have these murals everywhere, all over the republic. Every time we had a campaign to right some wrong, to reeducate the ignorant, art would be at the forefront."

"Ah, but that's what I mean, it could be the wrong way or the wrong direction. How can you control it once you've started?" he asked wisely.

Part Three

I admitted to Leopoldo that I wasn't sure. Although we continued to discuss this philosophically for many years, there was some irony in that Leopoldo later owned a number of works by Rivera, including a self-portrait, which, when he was much older, made him a wealthy man.

12

A Job

My scholarship from General Múgica was not enough.
I took a number of odd jobs during my years at the National
Preparatory School. I was able to sustain myself through
the remaining years and complete my preparatory education. However, when the governor's term ended, so did my
fellowship, and I found myself without a means of support.
After looking desperately for jobs, I finally was taken on
as an assistant to a paymaster for the Mexican Light and
Power Company, the major electrical firm in Mexico City.
To do this, I had to give up my educational plans and work
full-time.

The job thrust a lot of responsibility on me. We travelled
to numerous locations, arriving the day before the workmen
were paid. It was our function to pay the employees and keep
records of the transactions. I worked for several years as an
assistant until some fortuitous circumstances intervened and
changed my luck. On one occasion we had gone to a job location as usual. I had gotten up early to count in cash the salaries that were to be paid that morning. I was sitting in a ram-

shackle office making small piles of coins when a knock came on the door.

A man asked if I were Antonio Gutiérrez. When I told him I was, he informed me that my boss was quite ill and could not come to the office. The messenger further indicated that I should pay the workers myself. I thanked him for coming.

The man left. Stunned, I remained in my chair. I was to pay out hundreds of pesos myself. What if I made a mistake? We had to pay each man in pesos and centavos, which made it impossible to come out exactly correct. Usually my boss made up any difference in centavos against the company out of his own pocket. Thinking there was little chance for success, I decided I would continue making up more piles of coins in anticipation of the pay call. It was all I could do to maintain sufficient calm to continue with my regular procedure. Just before the dreaded hour arrived, the general manager entered the office.

He had heard about the situation. He wanted reassurance from me that I could handle the workers. For some reason, I didn't hesitate in my response. I told him I thought I could manage. He said he would stay and keep the lines orderly.

I thanked him for his help. I wasn't convinced that was the only reason he was staying, since I was handling considerable sums of money. It was a long morning of handing out coins to lines of laborers waiting patiently, hat in hand. As I approached the end of the line I became increasingly nervous about the monies not totaling up. But, to my utter astonishment, it came out to the centavo. The general manager was even more impressed.

I myself did not understand how I had done so well. Without comprehending it myself, I tried to explain my success to the manager.

"Whatever secrets you have, they work. You're young, but

I think you should have more responsibility," suggested the manager confidently.

Naturally, I told him I would like to have such an opportunity. He insisted that he would make it possible. I cautioned myself, not wanting unreasonably to raise my hopes. It occurred to me that the man was just flattering my ego. But, my doubts were unfounded.

Within a week I was told to report back to the main office, where I was given a position with greater responsibilities, but which didn't involve money. The management asked me to work on improving labor relations and to assist in handling labor complaints. I knew this would be a difficult position, but it was a promotion and paid well. I took it. For the first time in my life I had some extra money, money which I sent home to Purépero, to my mother and Camila. This new position also increased my social and political interests, and I began to subscribe to several newspapers. In particular, I paid close attention to the cartoonists of the 1920s, including the work of Fernando Leal, one of the early artists in the mural movement. One of his more striking illustrations portrayed a beggar with a scrawny dog and an outheld hat accosting a plump, well-dressed citizen with the accompanying conversation:

"A small alms for a poor, blind father."

"How many children do you have?" asked the well-dressed man.

"I do not know, my chief, I cannot see!"

Sometimes there we could find humor in our poverty, but more typically students and professional people discussed these problems and analyzed alternatives for solving them. The contrast between tradition and modernization, which had always been present in Mexico, became more pronounced in the city. I did most of my shopping in open stores then known as the El Volador Mercado. This commercial center gave the appearance of a Near Eastern market since the stalls were sheltered with sheets of white muslin. There, people sold and bartered goods brought to the city from distant locations. The rural dress of many of the traders contrasted sharply with the clothes of Mexico City urbanites, even those of unskilled laborers.

In the evenings I would go to El Gallo de Oro café with some of my newfound friends in the labor unions, although it remained a student hangout from my *prepa* days. Or, when my pockets were richer, I splurged at the Café Colón, a restaurant where almost any politician could be found at one time or another. We would argue about current political affairs, and, in our quieter moments, overhear snatches of conversations from other tables.

Working as a labor negotiator for Mexican Power and Light challenged my own developing political views more so than any of my previous experiences. My first job had been a question of survival, and I, like most other workers, saw myself as earning a living. Now, with my new position, I slowly began to see myself working for the interests of a company, interests that were not parallel to my own personal goals for Mexico. The 1920s set in motion a boom period of growth in the Mexican labor movement, represented nationally by the Regional Federation of Mexican Workers (CROM), then headed by Luis Morones. Although Mexican Power and Light used me to deal with the various skilled and unskilled workers with whom they contracted for certain projects, I became friends with several of the labor leaders I met frequently across the bargaining table. I socialized with these men and we discussed various issues related to our profession.

One of the political complications of the labor movement stemmed from the introduction of workers as a powerful political actor. When General Obregón confronted Carranza in his battle for control of the government, labor battalions came to his aid. But in the eyes of management, and in the view of many politicians, labor was becoming too powerful. The traditional actors in Mexico had been the army, the Church, and the landowners. Since the Revolution, the power of the Church and landowners had declined and the army had become increasingly important. The entrepreneurial class was weak and disorganized. Politicians were more likely to come from revolutionary backgrounds; many were from working class occupations; others were professionals, especially lawyers and, to a lesser extent, physicians and engineers.

Even union leaders themselves had differing views on labor's political role. One day, José Alarcón, a union leader, asked me if unions should stay out of politics. Because of my position, and my own feelings, I argued the pros and cons of that question. "My bosses would like to see that happen. It would make our relations with you more predictable. But maybe that is why your movement has grown."

He agreed, "But they have forgotten some of our reasons for organizing. We grouped together for better benefits, shorter workdays, and higher salaries. Now look at us. I think we need to decentralize. The big labor bosses try to manipulate us too, like your firm."

"I'm glad you think there is someone in your organization as bad as my firm," I joked. "But it's true labor has organizational problems. Why don't you declare your independence from CROM?"

"Do you think I'm crazy? Look at what has happened to Juan Escudero, or any labor leader who is too radical. Even their own treat them like black sheep."

I argued that there must be something they could do to increase their independence.

"Yeah, become the big cheese," interjected my second companion, Miguel Ortega, an ebullient but resourceful negotiator.

"Of what?" I asked.

"Take over the whole organization, then direct it wherever you want to go."

"Another Luis Morones," laughed José.

"Sure, don't fight the top, take it over," Miguel added.

"Well," I commented, "that's a very practical solution, but difficult to execute, especially if your moves are obvious."

José, flailing his sweat-stained arms, vociferously agreed. "That's just what your bosses would like, internal war. We have to stick together to beat those guys." He punctuated his words with a gulp of beer.

"Okay," I said, changing the subject, "let's discuss nonunion politics. What's Calles doing for the Mexicans?"

"What he's done with the Church is fine with me," replied José.

"That's for sure," added his companion, "but what about land reform?"

"He started off the same as Obregón, but he doesn't seem to be emphasizing collective holdings," I stated.

"You're right. He's stressing individual holdings, but at least to his credit he's doing something about irrigation and roads in rural areas, and he has given out larger plots than Obregón," responded José.

Miguel did not agree, at least with the positive tone of José's comments. "This may be, but what about the workers? Calles has crushed our movement. You'll be out of a job Toño. There aren't any more strikes. You can see the difference he's made in the labor movement."

After many more arguments and many more beers, the evening came to an end. Our arms intertwined, we moved unsteadily down the sidewalk, whistling at the women and bumping heavily into the walls, until we went our separate ways and with our differing viewpoints. Even in a light-headed state, I thought that despite Mexico's shortcomings, there was room for optimism in the future, a future which would see Mexico become a great country.

13

No Reelection

Nineteen twenty-seven was an important year for decisions in my life. It did not start out that way. My job was going well, I was rather successful at what I did, and I liked my professional friends. But I felt a persistent sense of restlessness, a desire for something else. I did not know what the missing element was until the year was nearly over. I continued to visit some of my student haunts. At one of these cafés, a conversation led to my involvement in events that changed my career.

One day I sat behind a small, wooden table covered with a blue and white checked cloth. A small, clay ashtray stained grey-black, piled high with crumpled cigarette wrappings, provided an uninviting setting. Beer stains covered the tablecloth. The popular strains of revolutionary music filtered through the doorway from a blind guitarist on the sidewalk outside. I was watching the activities at the other tables when some of my pals from *Eureka* walked in and headed toward me. In the lead was Amado, who was now in law school. They pulled out some chairs and sat down. Amado was anxious to talk to me. He was always inviting me to participate in one political activity or another. This time, he wanted me to join a group of supporters for General Arnulfo Gómez.

General Gómez was one of several prominent officers who had become enmeshed in the major political issue of the year when General Alvaro Obregón, who served as president of Mexico from 1920 to 1924, decided to break tradition and subvert the Constitution by running for another term in office. Since "Effective Suffrage and No Reelection" had been a widespread motto of the 1910 Revolution, and since Porfirio Díaz himself had initially used non-consecutive reelection as a means of continuing his influence over the presidency, many revolutionaries considered reelection of any sort an anathema. Obregón's enemies also used the reelection issue as a pretext to rally supporters opposed to his cause. I had never been an ardent admirer of Obregón, but unlike his critics, I believed he had accomplished much for Mexico. On the other hand, by tradition, I had been a strict constitutionalist since my days in Morelia under the guidance of my friend Andrés Bustamante. My contact with Múgica had also influenced my views on these issues. At this point I was miffed by Obregón's designs on the presidency, but I remained fairly neutral. I decided to see what arguments Amado could muster in support of his position.

I bluntly confronted him. "Why should I join you, Amado? After all, I have a job and Gómez is just another general."

"He's a general, no doubt about that, but at least he would be independent of the sly continuation of the Obregón-Calles dominance of the presidency."

I agreed with him, but I had my doubts about Gómez's ability to govern.

"I think he has as much ability as Obregón," Amado continued, "and at least he's sympathetic to the public's feelings.

We cannot allow each president to subvert the Constitution in his own interests. Before long, the Constitution will become a meaningless document. We have to defend a principle. You believe in that, don't you?"

I replied I had held that principle since my youth in Morelia, but I couldn't make a decision right away. Amado explained that his group was only beginning to be organized, and if I should decide to join in the next few weeks, my participation would be welcome. We continued to discuss the matter at some length. I pondered my course of action for several days after the meeting. Because I felt a strong desire to become involved, I easily let myself be convinced, not so much by the political arguments, but by my desire to be part of a national campaign.

Most of the supporters in our immediate group were *prepas* and law students. Because of my contact with labor leaders I was asked to make speeches to labor groups in support of General Gómez's candidacy. This was somewhat difficult among organized labor since Luis Morones, their major national leader, had political ambitions for the presidency and was supported by labor-political organizations. My political activities were confined to evenings after work and weekends. My oratory skills improved, but perhaps more important, I became friends with several acquaintances from my *prepa* days, including Miguel Alemán, about whom I learned a great deal. Our friendship began after I had delivered a speech to a small gathering of laborers.

We discussed similarities and differences between our boyhood experiences in Veracruz and Michoacán. After preparatory school, Miguel had continued his education at the national law school. He brought me up-to-date on his other activities. I was curious about his reasons for supporting Gómez's campaign.

"My support of Gómez stems partly from the principle of

allowing opposition candidates to express their political views and provide an alternative to Obregón's candidacy. You've heard of my father?"

I replied that I had.

Miguel explained, "He holds strong political views, and my family has suffered because of his activities. I don't think people should suffer because of what they or their parents believe. My father has opposed Obregón politically for some time because he's abusing the Constitution."

Here our views corresponded. We also shared an interest in labor groups and their working conditions. Miguel planned to write his law thesis on miners and their problems.

At first the campaign seemed to be going well. Obregón was well liked, yet we continued to attract support for General Gómez, who received favorable press coverage and whose rallies were well attended. The campaign became more complicated when General Francisco Serrano, another former ally of Obregón, also decided to run for office. I disliked Serrano, who unlike Gómez, had been a profligate spender under Obregón's personal protection. Some of our more important leaders tried to reach an agreement with Serrano's supporters, whereby one of the candidates would drop out of the race, but nothing came of it.

At that point, I began to be discouraged. I wasn't a full-time campaigner because, of course, I had to work. In addition, I had no sense of the ordinary person's support for Gómez since I usually remained in Mexico City and, except for an occasional speech to labor groups, had little contact with the general public because I normally worked at campaign headquarters. I was discouraged with the inability of the two opposition groups to either agree on a third candidate to oppose Obregón, or to join together. I would not have been enthusiastic about supporting Serrano since I believed him to be corrupt and immature. Nevertheless, I was willing to sacrifice my feelings toward Serrano in order to strengthen opposition to Obregón. When all of the collaborative efforts failed, I finally realized that we were unable to give greater loyalty to a concept or idea than to a political figure. Over and over again this was to be our downfall. No one on either side was willing to compromise to defend the principle of no reelection.

Various factions supported Gómez. I was more strongly identified with the Anti-Reelectionist group than with Gómez himself. One of our campaign pledges was to pay more attention to the agrarian problem, especially to provide assistance for the ejido program. President Calles awarded some landless peasants their own lands, although the pace of his reform paled before that of General Obregón. Yet, neither Obregón nor Calles gave the peasants sufficient credit to make their property productive. Had we had the opportunity to implement a better-funded agrarian program, the whole future of the Mexican economy would have been altered.

As the campaigns progressed, rumors of possible military revolts in support of successful candidates abounded. By late September, these rumors reached us daily. At that time, I had my first opportunity to see General Arnulfo Gómez in the flesh. When he spoke to a small group of volunteer workers, he looked like a well-dressed businessman. While not a charismatic speaker, he was a handsome figure. He had dark hair combed back off his forehead and brows that arched slightly over an aquiline nose. Throughout his talk, although visibly tired, he maintained a sense of humor.

A week later on October 3, our hopes and those of the two candidates were abruptly shattered. The Mexico City newspapers announced the execution of General Serrano and a number of his prominent supporters on the road to Cuernavaca. I immediately contacted some of my co-workers at the Gómez campaign headquarters. General Gómez, catching wind of the government's decision to treat opposition candi-

dates as leaders of military rebellions, anticipated further violence and fled to Veracruz, where he hoped to meet friendly
troops. As minor civilian participants, we were unlikely to be
persecuted and were thus advised to remain in Mexico City
and continue our normal affairs.

A number of generals revolted against the government, but
their attempts were tardy and disorganized. Many took advantage of the disorder to settle old, personal scores. General
Gómez succeeded in organizing a small army in Veracruz, but
his efforts were fruitless. Pursued by progovernment army
troops, he was defeated and fled to the mountains. One month
later, having been betrayed as were so many revolutionary
leaders before him, he was captured and executed. On November 6th, his body arrived by train in Mexico City. We were
allowed a public burial, and Vito Alessio Robles, a long-
standing antireelectionist and a leading supporter of Gómez's
campaign, gave the funeral oration. It was a moving and patriotic speech. He argued that antireelectionism was not dead.

Some of my friends nearly ended up the same way as our
candidate. Miguel Alemán had several close calls, probably
because of his father. He fled Mexico City and, under a safe-
conduct pass from a family friend, made his way back to Veracruz where he received the protection of officers friendly to
his father. It was several months before he could return safely
to Mexico City and continue his law courses.

After many years, I can look back on this event with somewhat more objectivity than I could then. Obregón always
claimed that neither Gómez nor Serrano had the capacity to
govern Mexico. He implied that his personal leadership was
necessary to lead Mexico through these difficult years. I'm
now willing to admit that he may have been right, and that
Serrano, unconcerned with what the public wanted, pushed
Obregón into a military solution. But, I still believe my generation went into the campaign with a false sense of security.

Part Three

We believed sincerely in democracy. We deceived ourselves into thinking that the Constitution would remain inviolate, and that the only task before us was to persuade the Mexican people to support our candidate. The rules of democracy in those days, unfortunately, were tenuous. Force decided political outcomes. I think, however, through bitter experience, we understood the gap between what we wanted for Mexico, and what characterized our politics in the late 1920s. This lesson learned from the 1927 campaign produced much fruit in succeeding decades.

The tragic end to my second experience in politics jarred me from my daily routine as a labor negotiator. As I took on more responsibility in this position, I soon had a sizable staff working under me, including several lawyers. I became increasingly embarrassed by my lack of formal education as I supervised others more educated than myself. I resolved that once the campaign was completed, I would figure out a way to return to school. Of course, the campaign's end had come sooner than I expected. I decided to ask Alessio Robles for his advice. He agreeably conceded to give me an interview.

Vito Alessio Robles was a portly man whose most prominent feature was his tortoiseshell eyeglasses. His political activities were endless, for he and his brother Miguel had been involved in politics since the first decade of the twentieth century. Aside from his political interests he was quite knowledgeable about the National University and had many friends there. It was said that he had been spared the same fate as General Gómez because President Calles's and Robles's daughters were close friends.

When I arrived at his home I expressed my desire to enroll in the university. When he asked me why I hadn't already done so, I explained that I didn't have enough money to support myself in school, and asked if I might obtain a scholarship. He expressed sympathy toward my predicament, but before he would commit himself to helping me, he asked a series of questions. He questioned me about my preparatory education; I told him I had completed it in Mexico City. He also wanted to know my field of interest. In those days, most students pursued law or medicine, and a smaller group followed the engineering discipline. I told him I was interested in law. He made no promises, but implied that he would speak with the dean about helping me. I thanked him profusely.

"It is nothing," he said, patting me on the shoulder. "I'm trying to do as much as possible for those who served our cause. Many have had difficulties retaining their jobs. Perhaps we'll have another opportunity to take the campaign trail together."

I told him I hoped that we would. We talked about political affairs for a long time, and when I finally left, it was quite late. As the servant shut the door behind me, I found myself on a deserted sidewalk. Disoriented, I stepped into the street, only to be suddenly jolted and twisted around by the friction of a square, black sedan whizzing by. Completely preoccupied by my future as a *universitario*, I had forgotten to pay attention. A longer or quicker step would have ended that dream forever.

14

The School
of Law

Long rows of buses and trolleys blocked my path across the
Zócalo, their rectangular bodies standing end to end in the
sun. Each bus looked like a truck, its stubby engine housing in
the front, straddled by large headlights and curved, prominent
fenders. The windshields were square, and stood perpendicular to the hood, like the windows of a home or office building.
Simple wooden seats ran parallel to the body of the chassis.
Passengers faced inward looking across at each other. It was
warm, so the shades were rolled up to the roof. The side window frames contained no glass. The ride wasn't smooth, but it
was much easier to see the streets and sights from a bus then
than it is from today's buses. Actually, the trolleys were faster
and more comfortable, but they travelled to only a few locations. They looked like the passenger cars of a train except
they had doors on the side and the windows in front.

I worked my way through the people searching for buses
or trolleys that would take them to the right location. What a
contrast to my native village! I never had seen such machines
until I came to Mexico City. For me, the machine age had ar-

rived. Truly this was progress. Mexico and its capital city underwent many changes during the 1920s. In the distance I could see the Monument to the Revolution, a structure which, because of its great height, dominated most of the surrounding blocks. It was the highest building I had ever seen. Its construction, totally unfunctional, allowed people to walk underneath much like the Eiffel tower.

I took various routes daily to my law classes. The school building was nothing like the Preparatory School, which had much more personality. But many of my professors were young, had revolutionary ideas, and taught law as though we were the only generation who could rebuild Mexico's legal and administrative structure. It had been more than a year since I gave up the security of my job to work for a law degree. I had no regrets. Law school exposed me to several subjects I had not taken before: economics and sociology. Some of the most notable essayists, scholars, and political leaders of the 1920s became our professors. Alessio Robles hadn't let me down, and through his help I succeeded in obtaining a work scholarship and another part-time job as a janitor at the Law School.

My favorite professors at the Law School usually were those who were or who had been in public service. They flavored their lectures with spicy examples from public careers. During my second year I was particularly impressed with the classes given by Manuel Gómez Morín, perhaps the leading contributor to the creation of Mexico's banking system in the 1920s and early 1930s. He had a brilliant and incisive mind, and dominated the classroom. I did well in his classes, and he accepted me as a protégé. We initiated a friendship because we had certain experiences in common. Like me, my mentor had grown up in a rural environment, but in northern Mexico. More important, his father had died when he was young, leaving him to support his mother after their inheritance ran out. I guess he felt a certain sympathy for me after learning about my own situation. Further, as a young lawyer, he had participated in an unsuccessful rebellion against the government led by General Adolfo de la Huerta in 1923. At the tender age of twenty-two he served as Subsecretary of the National Treasury Department, the youngest man ever to have held that position. His intense interest in political affairs rubbed off on me, but I was not his only favorite. He attracted many students, and on his way to and from class he constantly engaged in conversation with one or more admirers.

One day before class started, several of my classmates and I discussed the agrarian reform program in Mexico, a topic of much interest. Amado Cosío, my former companion from *Eureka* was also present since he, too, as a fifth-year law student, was taking this course, which was an elective.

"We need to go back to the collective concept of agriculture like our native ancestors if a permanent reform of land distribution is to succeed," he said.

Mario Silvestre, another companion, quickly responded, "The trouble with you, Amado, is that you are always proposing the collective solution. The Liberals of the nineteenth century were right, you can't develop the rural areas if the land is held jointly. There isn't any incentive to produce."

"We do not have any evidence of that, Mario," argued Amado, "and besides, if we individualize all of that property, we are going to have more problems."

"Such as . . . ," interrupted Mario.

"For one thing, remember what happened to the Liberal program when they tried to force the sale of village-held land. The Indians and peasants are ignorant and lack the ability to develop their land sufficiently. If they have title to the land, it will soon be sold and acquired by other interests."

"But there are legal limitations as to what each person can have," I replied.

"You're so naïve," countered Amado. "Do you think these

provisions will help? They're about as effective as our laws requiring mandatory primary education. Nothing is ever enforced. Even if the land laws were followed families could control more land than the law permits merely by putting holdings under the names of individual family members, including children."

"Maybe this would happen," I admitted, not yet willing to give in, "but you still haven't explained how collective land will be productive. People need a personal incentive. That's the way human beings are. You or anyone else can't change that with some theoretical argument."

"I don't agree, Toño; people can change their attitudes and behavior. Representatives of the government, the agrarian agencies, and teachers need to reeducate the people. Give them a sense of unity. Unity to help each other. The Russians are doing this aren't they? Why can't we?" he replied, rubbing the inside of his collar with his index finger.

I thought for a few moments and then continued. "Well, the Russians may be doing that, but the liberty they have is much more restricted than ours. It goes back to your point about mandatory education. If nothing is enforced, then how can everyone be affected by an idea or belief? Some people change, and some don't. We don't have the moral authority or the force to bring about a change in thought. Still, one should ask, have the Russians succeeded?" I paused, "What I mean is, maybe they've collectivized thought, but what about their agricultural productivity? They're not doing very well, are they?"

Amado's chair scraped against the floor as he readjusted his weight and turned to face a growing audience of fellow students. "The statistics we read in the newspapers are always biased. They are not an accurate reflection of the truth of the Soviet experiment. The collective approach would make it possible for peasants to use machinery by enlarging their plots. If they work hard, they will find incentive in the profit to be made through cooperative effort, a profit divided among the members and reinvested in the land. Then, individually poor farmers will have the same opportunity for new machinery and fertilizers as the rich *hacendados*. We're not removing all incentives like the Soviets, only making it a group incentive."

I remained unconvinced. "It's a good argument, Amado, but where will they get the credit to buy tools and products for the land? Who among the *campesinos* understands their use? It would take several generations. Meanwhile, are we city dwellers to starve? Or, do we turn to the gringos up North for food? That would really be bad."

"I . . ."

"He's coming," someone yelled from the back, referring to Professor Gómez Morín.

Quickly, everyone straightened in their chairs and looked toward the front. We were very orderly and formal in those days, and that was how we were expected to greet our instructors. Gómez Morín walked with a quick step to the front of the class. Although normally he lectured, we did hold a class discussion related to the lecture's subject matter. Toward the end of the class, Amado asked Gómez Morín if he would comment on the agrarian problem we had discussed earlier. He elucidated the difficulties of each approach to solving Mexico's rural problems, but one of his arguments remained fixed in my mind, that of Mexico's lack of organization. He criticized the state for not developing efficient institutions to organize and manage programs essential to Mexico's development. He would bring up this theme time and time again.

In 1929, one of Gómez Morín's friends from preparatory school, an individual who would become equally well known in political affairs of the 1930s—Narciso Bassols—became dean of the Law School. Gómez Morín asked him to continue and to increase my financial assistance. Bassols kindly assented to this request, until 1931, when he left the deanship. By then, I too had reached my last year in Law School and, through my continued association with Gómez Morín, had become his assistant. What an honor! There I was, a mere student helping to teach his classes. Such assistantships were not common. My function was to take classes when he could not teach because of professional obligations or illness and to answer questions from the students in occasional discussion sessions.

To be challenged by younger students in a teaching situation built up my confidence and improved my analytical skills. Equally important was my contact with underclassmen. Many of these younger students became close friends, and their friendships were important in later years. But law school was not an entirely placid academic or gay social experience. Two important events intruded on my student career, and these were abrupt, additional steps in my political initiation.

1 5

A Strike

The pings developed into a pleasing and regular melody as water drops fell from the faucet. I moved my legs and the tone immediately changed. Reaching up with my left foot, I grasped the pronged handle between my big and second toe, adding more hot water to the tub. It seeped into the already tepid water, reaching my buttocks and back last. I slid the rear of my body downward to absorb more of its warmth against the morning cold. I had splurged that day by adding powdered bubble bath to the water. It expanded quickly and enveloped my legs, reaching the rust stains that hung like brown beards below the chrome faces of the bath fixtures. At that moment, I felt like going back to sleep in the warm, watery bed. This was a habit I developed in my twenties; soaking in the tub was a time for contemplation of visions—aesthetic, social, and political. I made plans and decisions about my future. In later years when my schedule was hectic, it was the time reserved for myself, a time every successful politician must have, but so difficult to acquire.

Instead of succumbing to the warmth, I grasped the curved

rims of the tub, stood up, and grabbed my towel off a nearby stool. I dried the middle part of my torso first, then reached down and rubbed my toes, feet, and ankles. Last, I touseled my hair and pulled the towel down over the nape of my neck. I took my father's cup from a shelf over the sink, and adding some hot water, I began swirling my brush until the bristles were covered with lather. I watched myself in the mirror and dabbed the runny mixture over my face.

It would be a hard decision to make, I thought. Many students, including a good number of my friends, had decided to call a strike in May 1929 against the rector of the National University, Antonio Castro Leal. They were protesting a change in our program that would require law students and other professional students to take written examinations. Prior to the ruling we had taken only an oral exam. Actually, I thought the oral examination was more threatening than any written test someone might conjure up. At the same time I had good feelings about the Law School dean, Narciso Bassols, who had helped me to stay in school. There were other changes dealing with the school calendar and the curriculum, but these were less important. Should I join my friends? I wrestled with the decision and finally concluded that friendship was more important than other considerations, so I joined their cause. I wanted to wait and see if our declaration of a general strike would produce results. What we really wanted was the right to be heard and represented on these issues, rather than have them unilaterally declared by administrators. This was not so different from what happened to students in other parts of the world in the 1960s.

The next day the law students declared a general strike. Instead of making concessions, the President of Mexico, attempting to avoid more conflict, closed down the University. This actually proved to be a boon to our cause. A number of prominent student leaders, particularly Salvador Azuela, son of the famous Mexican novelist, and Alejandro Gómez Arias, a great orator, joined us. They both were leaders of the national student congresses held in the 1920s, and their support encouraged other student leaders throughout Mexico to join our movement.

Since we could not occupy the Law School building, student leaders at the National Preparatory School permitted us to use their building as a base of operations. Interested students met there, and we debated a number of demands, which we later formulated into resolutions. We also elected a strike committee, of which I became a member. The next day I took a petition to all the student haunts, trying to get students to sign a document stating they would not attend class. I obtained help from Leopoldo Vela, who by that time was a practicing physician and a young professor at the Medical School.

We were quite successful and secured hundreds of student signatures. Most fulfilled their promise not to attend class. But the next day we decided to demonstrate publicly against the administration's policies. We marched down several blocks, but police and firemen prevented us from moving farther. After shouting and accusations from both sides, the police began swinging their clubs. Students in the streets and in nearby buildings responded by throwing paving stones. We were like two surging waves, first we would charge them, hurling a barrage of stones, then they would beat back our charge, raining blows on our backs and shoulders and cracking heads. I barely stayed ahead of their clubs. I felt sorry for the police. They were pawns in the hands of their chief. Most were from poor mestizo families, with ill-fitting uniforms and little training. At first they seemed reluctant. But the heat of battle soon encouraged all participants to vent their frustrations, personal and otherwise, on each other. Once the melee reached its peak, they became, even to me, the enemy.

It was during one of the retreats that I stumbled across Amadito, lying on the ground, weakly trying to protect his head. Blood seeped through his fingers and stained the front of his shirt.

I cried out to him.

He mumbled something I could not hear.

I told him to put his head in my lap so I could examine the cut. Beneath the movement of students and police, I shifted his head around and shielded him from tripping feet. I nearly fainted when I lifted his hand from the left side of his head. His hair was matted and soaked with streaming blood. I took out my handkerchief, and pressing it downward with my palm, I placed his hand over the wound and told him to keep it there.

"Look," I commanded, "we're going to have to get out of here."

Hesitantly, he agreed, but he was quite dizzy.

I threaded my hands under both shoulders and, clasping my fingers together, I pulled him up to my chest and stood up, holding him beneath me in an awkward half-crouch. At a moment when the students had surged forward, I steered through the screaming, raging mass. Amado's feet hung limply and dragged along the street between my legs. We had made some progress when I heard a shout close up and felt a sharp pain in my ribs. A policeman had approached on my blind side jamming his nightstick into me like a short battering ram. I tumbled forward, letting go of Amado to maintain my balance. The policeman was also thrown slightly off balance in giving the blow, and I used those few seconds to pick up a loose stone from the street. He towered over me. Turning quickly but remaining on one knee, I swung the stone with great force at the man's kneecap. It connected sharply. I had used such force that my own hand ached from the blow. The man cried out in pain and dropped his club. Without turning back to see his condition, I regrasped Amado and dragged

him farther away. Finally, almost completely out of breath and smarting from the blow to my ribs and hand, I was near collapse when two other students came to my assistance.

They carried Amado out of range. On a nearby street I hailed a taxi. One of our more foresighted leaders had persuaded several medical students to set up an aid station at a rooming house. We took Amado there, where he received caring, if not totally expert, attention. Students filled the room. Police brutality led to many complaints to the government. Several days later the President of Mexico asked students to explain their demands to him personally. He rejected our first set of requests but asked us to provide more reasons for our demands and to emphasize complaints against policy rather than against personalities.

The President's request forced us to reconsider our position and ultimately to articulate a broader goal, that of University autonomy. We addressed our ideas to the President once again. With his collaboration, we produced a document that in theory, anyway, removed the government's control over the University. In practice this was never entirely the case, but we felt we had achieved a major victory over the government. As a result of the strike and the negotiations, the leadership of the university and of the law school did change. We celebrated our victory in cafés and student rooming houses for days.

But the University strike and the autonomy we ultimately achieved were not the only issues affecting students and professors in 1929. In 1928, after Obregón successfully eliminated his most effective opponents, he won the election. He was assassinated by a fanatic at a banquet in a Mexico City restaurant, while celebrating his electoral victory. Thus, Mexico found itself without a successor to replace General Calles, the retiring president. The Constitution specifies that in this situation Congress should appoint an interim president and a new election should be held. It was obvious that Calles exerted some influence over their decision. After considerable discussion, Congress chose Emilio Portes Gil, the president responsible for granting us autonomy.

At the same time, government leaders needed to select a new candidate to represent them in the special presidential election of 1929. Some of my friends thought Calles had something to do with the assassination of Obregón, but I always believed that he was murdered by a religious fanatic, not a political assassin. President Calles himself revived religious fanaticism, and the simmering conflict between the Catholic Church and the state, a latent issue from the nineteenth century that was rekindled by the Revolution. Of course, the 1917 Constitution included many restrictive provisions against the clergy and the Church. Obregón had not initiated their enforcement. But Calles, who took a more anticlerical stance, confronted the Church head on. On the state level, groups sympathetic to the Church rallied behind it. In the second half of Calles's term, peasants led by pro-Catholic leaders in west central Mexico launched a full-fledged rebellion against the government. Newspapers reported attacks by guerrilla bands on trains and government troops, their battle cry of "Long Live Christ the King" prominent in the headlines.

In Mexico City, we didn't pay much attention to this issue, despite its serious consequences for many states, including my beloved Michoacán. The vast majority of the students were neutral concerning the Cristeros, or unsympathetic to the position of the Church. The proclerical student faction grew much stronger in the 1930s. Whereas most of us didn't favor repressive measures taken by some state governors against the clergy, notably Garrido Canabal in Tabasco, we were definitely committed to the Liberal principle of state supremacy over the Church. This attitude was so pervasive that any student wishing to pursue a successful political career in the 1930s would not have advertised his Catholicism; political leadership was not sympathetic to a pro-Catholic view. Some members of my generation, who remained in the provinces, were actively pro-Cristero, especially a group from Guadalajara, a hotbed of pro-clerical activity. One such student, Agustín Yáñez, later my friend and one of our distinguished novelists, abandoned his fervent support of the Catholic Youth Movement. By coming to Mexico City in the 1930s and making a name for himself as an intellectual first, he ultimately achieved a position of national leadership as a politician.

Perhaps we were somewhat myopic in ignoring this issue. Life in Mexico City filtered out and distorted issues important to the provinces. We had begun to come under the influence of an intellectual trend in which the city captivated and molded our views from an urban, cosmopolitan angle. This urban blindness, as I later learned, eventually became a political illness, which we have yet to cure. The disease has spread to such an extent that few of today's leaders can interpret regional issues without a jaundiced view. But I am willing to admit that my own group was one of the first to contract this disease, one which we passed on to successive generations of leaders.

I expected Calles to pick someone with more national appeal to serve as a candidate in the new election, even though it appeared he wanted to remain in control of the political situation. Instead, he selected a little-known engineer and politician from my home state, Pascual Ortiz Rubio, the very same figure who had opposed Múgica. During most of the recent political events, Ortiz Rubio had been out of the country serving as our ambassador to Brazil. It became obvious to most of us who opposed the Obregón-Calles clique that Calles wanted someone he could control. To give legitimacy to this new candidacy, and to create a facade behind which he could hide, Calles organized a national party to represent his political philosophy. This party became known as the Party of the Mexican Revolution (later the PRI).

Many student activists and political leaders who had opposed Obregón in 1927–28 once again decided to oppose the government candidate in 1929. Leading that opposition was a man who emerged as a key figure in the first Obregón administration—José Vasconcelos. Many of my friends and I saw Vasconcelos, who headed the Ministry of Public Education in the early 1920s, as an honest and creative administrator who had contributed greatly to Mexican education and culture. It was not long before support for his candidacy grew among former antireelectionists, students, and even participants in some of the abortive campaigns prior to 1927. Once again, I was drawn directly into politics.

16

Los
Vasconcelistas

The man spat quietly. His spittle shot across the road, picking up dust as it rolled to a stop and dissolved into the surface. As far as the eye could see the spiny leaves of the henequen plant reached for the sky. My guide, whose soiled, white peasant pajamas hung loosely around his body, motioned toward a small path leading from the road over a hump of weeds and soil through the plants. I followed him into their protective shadows. The sun was still low and the morning's moisture had already disappeared from the parched leaves. I averted my eyes from the plants to the path we were taking, and then to the guide's feet. They were wrinkled from sun and abuse. He had large cracks in the backs of his heels. His toenails were split and filled with dirt. He didn't avoid stepping on the various rocks protruding from the soft dust of the path. I had already wisely exchanged my city shoes for *huaraches* in this hot, tropical climate.

In 1929, Yucatán was a remote corner of Mexico—distant in time and culture from Mexico City. I had joined the Vasconcelos campaign and, after some initial activities in the capital city,

115

was sent to southern Mexico to appeal to some newly organized agrarian groups for support of our candidate. At that time there was no train to Mérida, the colonial capital of this restless peninsula. I took a train as far as Veracruz, then a combination of buses down the coast through Tabasco and Campeche. I had to ride numerous ferries over the inland lagoons, delaying travel for many hours. There were certain advantages to this, among which were the tasty shrimp I purchased at many of the ferry sites. As a native of landlocked Michoacán, my being exposed to the sea, particularly the clear, light greens and blues of southern Mexico, was a remarkable experience. I also used some of the time at these stops to walk the beaches, picking up dozens of colorful, ornate shells washed in by the Caribbean waters.

Mérida was an interesting provincial city. Spanish colonial architecture still retained a firm hold on the structural flavor of the community. Pre-Revolutionary wealth was astounding. Ornate plastered colonial mansions stood on spacious grounds. Carefully pruned bermuda grass carpeted the yards. Each shrub or tree received meticulous, individual care. The whitewash was freshly redone to prevent the mold which thrived in this climate and quickly crept over the outside of most homes. Many homes were fronted with high, black enameled ironwork; while others, hidden from view by thick walls had to be left to the imagination. These residences' maintenance required great wealth and labor. Although many of the *hacendados* had been destroyed by the ravages of the Revolution, others survived by transferring their resources into urban real estate, leaving their homes to be taken over by the new crop of political leaders emerging in the 1920s.

I initiated my campaign efforts outside the city in the small but important port town of Progreso, where ships from New Orleans, Havana, and Puerto Barrios docked to exchange goods. The pro-Vasconcelos committee in Mérida asked me to

speak to fishermen and dockworkers. The ride from Mérida
to Progreso, which I made in a narrow-gauge, puffing train,
opened my eyes to the economic base of Yucatán—henequen.
This plant produced sisal, the rope used around the world for
shipping and dockwork. We passed many peasants of Mayan
descent walking along the roadbed with a machete in one
hand and a small pouch of tortillas, their lunch, in the other.
Tied to their belts were old liquor bottles filled with water.

My urban appearances, such as the visit to Progreso, were
few. Instead, I found myself on henequen plantations, visiting
workers in the field. This morning my silent guide was leading me to small groups of workers laboring at various tasks.
As we continued along the path, I began to hear the slashing
sounds of machetes biting into the green flesh of the plants.
When we were at arm's length from the harvested henequen,
the plants looked like recently pruned palm trees, their large,
lower spines trimmed off neatly at the base of each stalk.
Where each missing leaf had previously joined the plant a
bright, white colored splotch appeared. Neatly piled stacks of
leaves with the spines pointing all the same direction lay at
the foot of every three to four plants. The harvested plants
seemed naked. I learned that they could be cultivated only for
a few years; then the field was burned, allowed to lie fallow
awhile, and then replanted.

I could see the men now. They were conversing in Mayan
with a sprinkling of Spanish words. The chattering quieted
as they heard us arrive and familiar greetings welcomed my
guide. For most city workers it was still a time of sleep. But
since the open fields exposed laborers to the sun's beating
rays, I addressed these workers very early, saving my talk to
those who worked around the hacienda buildings for last.
After a few words of introduction, and some nods of recognition from several of the workers, I spoke about Vasconcelos,
and the alternatives he offered these people as a presidential

117

candidate. Much of what I had to say about my candidate involved political liberty, a commodity increasingly difficult to find in Mexico during those years. I spoke informally, leaning up against a natural wall of stones. Afterwards, several of the men asked me questions. We then took time out for tortillas and water before the men returned to their work.

In my own enthusiasm for Vasconcelos, I couldn't easily detect their response to my candidate or his ideals. Like most of my friends, I could truly believe in Vasconcelos. He conveyed a moral authority to us, but he appealed to most Mexicans on an intellectual level. Middle-class, urban residents responded to his criticism of the moral failures of the post-revolutionary leadership and their legacy of immorality that continues to plague us. But his political and social ideas were vague. Instead, he talked about changing our national character, especially our inability to compromise. In his speeches he preached to his listeners that they must forego their ill will toward others, replacing it with a trusting and generous attitude.

Vasconcelos was correct in his analysis of our character, but Mexicans, especially peasants, expected bread and butter issues. Instead, when he accepted the candidacy of the National Anti-Reelectionist Party, Vasconcelos launched a noble but unrealistic program. Among his ideals that we as students favored was devoting nearly a fourth of the budget to education. On agrarian reform, I could appeal to the ordinary farm worker since Vasconcelos favored strict support for the land-distribution program. But, because he didn't favor the involvement of politicians, especially agrarian leaders in the actual process, he lost the support of these important local figures.

On the broader political landscape, his program was even more illusory. Again, I found it appealing because he believed in effective suffrage, and in delegating greater authority to the Chamber of Deputies. But in a country where the president al-

ways had dominated political institutions, to advocate more power to the legislative branch was unrealistic. Vasconcelos went further, suggesting reducing the power of the army, which at that time completely dominated political life.

At the far end of the field some workers already had started to load the stems onto a flatbed railroad car. Instead of being connected to an engine, the car was hitched to a pair of mules. I helped the men stack the piles of henequen on the bed. When we finished the job I hopped on the rear, dangling my legs over the narrow-gauge track shiny from use. A driver and his assistant, standing near the front, untied the reins and with a snap of leather, the car lurched forward. The speed was quite remarkable as we travelled through the immense fields on our way back to the hacienda. Occasionally we stopped to open and close gates as we passed through. After thirty minutes we crossed the main highway and entered the hacienda grounds.

The buildings were patterned after the traditional Spanish colonial architecture. Most visitors entered through an ornate gate of stone and plaster covered with a faded coat of peeling, pink paint. From this gate, a wall extended in both directions. On the left stood the main house, an elongated rectangle with many bedrooms facing the interior. On the right, the wall ran for some distance before it joined a store where local workers purchased their supplies. The 1917 Constitution had outlawed company stores; but this one, now leased by one of the more prosperous local residents, stood in the same place as the previous landowner's store and no doubt the indebtedness of peasants persisted. In the background a row of huts built in Mayan style formed a perpendicular line. It was a place of constant activity as children played and their mothers went about household chores.

The tracks we followed came in from the left, parallel to the main house, making a graceful curve in the center of a grass-covered yard, before heading away from the front entryway. On this side, several buildings used to repair the flatcars and other machinery, or store supplies, formed another man-made barrier. The driver slowed the mules as we approached two other cars filled with neatly stacked stems. The car jerked to an uneven stop and the driver jumped down. I got off as they began to unhitch the mules. After guiding them away from the track, we pushed the car closer to those already sitting on the siding. Farther up the track stood a partially empty car next to a loading dock. The dock provided one side of a large archway to a building with several smokestacks and exposed machinery.

Since I had some free time before my next talk, I followed the tracks to the loading dock to see how the stalks were processed. There I could see several men unload the henequen and lay it on a large belt operated by a series of pulleys attached to the main machinery. This belt carried the leaves to a machine that split them apart, separating the fleshy green covering from the stark, white fibers inside. These fibers were cleaned and hung on row after row of wooden racks in an area behind the factory. After drying in the sun, the fibers could then be formed into rope. Some of the local workers braided the fibers by hand into 1/4-inch rope, to be sold or exchanged for other goods. The entire process used little machinery, and that which was there had been acquired before the turn of the century.

The social conditions of the people I talked to seemed little changed since 1920. I was surprised that the landowner allowed me to talk to his workers, but he was a supporter of Vasconcelos, and hoped that I would encourage his workers to support his candidate.

This was the first of many similar experiences I had in Yucatán. And although my youth made me an enthusiastic supporter of Vasconcelos, I gradually saw that intellectual training, honesty, and support for political liberty were not qualities dearest to the henequen workers. Prior to the Revolution their condition as laborers had been one of the worst in Mexico. They wanted economic and social reforms, not the right to vote. Their reaction was polite, not enthusiastic, except in urban areas. Nevertheless, in their efforts to prevent the people from hearing Vasconcelos's views, supporters of the government party provoked violence against our supporters reminiscent of my experiences with Múgica and Gómez.

When the election was held, Vasconcelos lost overwhelmingly. The vote tallies were surely dishonest. But, I'm not sure if they had been honest the results would have been different. Most of Vasconcelos's support came from students, the urban middle class, and conservatives who hoped to regain their position in society. Admirably, unlike so many losing candidates before him, he wasn't tempted to call for an armed rebellion, further depreciating nonviolent political solutions. It was a depressing period in my life. Vasconcelos himself never recovered his former prestige. Instead of remaining true to the major precepts of the Revolution, to our amazement, he became quite conservative. He moved away from the traditional Liberal posture, favoring a pro-Catholic position in the 1930s. As he did so, Vasconcelos distanced himself from his youthful supporters, I among them. My disappointment translated itself into disillusionment with the political system. I was on the losing side, but I made great gains in my political maturity. Maybe eventually my luck would change.

Part Four

A
Public Career
1933 – 1939

17

A Professional

In the late spring of 1932 I graduated with honors from the Law School. I remember that year like yesterday. By completing my degree I joined a very small group of Mexicans and, like most graduates, the only problem on my mind was that of securing a job. As was true for many of my friends, one of my professors helped me.

Early that June I received a message from Professor Gómez Morín to stop by his law office. When I went to see him, he offered me a job. To have a job was a cause for much personal satisfaction, but a job with Gómez Morín deserved a celebration. That I accomplished without any inhibitions.

The next day I embarked on a rewarding apprenticeship to my former professor, learning over the next several years how to apply my academic training to concrete legal situations. Most of our business concerned questions of civil and commercial disputes between private citizens and government agencies, or among individuals. I didn't handle criminal cases. Still, I explored new areas, and different personalities always made the cases interesting.

Part Four

Gómez Morín's office served as a gathering place for intellectuals. I met many important public figures in his office and became well acquainted with younger professionals, often his former students, who worked in government or in private practice. We weren't short of topics to discuss, for although a semblance of political stability had returned to Mexico since Pascual Ortiz Rubio's election, his unexpected resignation from the presidency in 1932 raised many questions in the press. In his place, Abelardo Rodríguez, a lesser-known general from northern Mexico, and an ally of Calles, took over the executive office.

In the fall of 1933 I became a professor at the Law School. I taught two courses, one in constitutional writs and the other in political economy, the latter a subject that recently had been transferred from Law to the new School of Economics. Perhaps because of my youth, students were attracted to me, and my class on political economy became the site of vigorous debates on Mexican policy. But the University itself could not be kept out of politics, and in this same year, a long-simmering issue came to a head on campus. The dispute centered on the question of academic freedom and the politicization of the curriculum.

Like many issues in Mexican politics, the broader significance was hidden behind more parochial questions and dominant personalities. Two of the leaders who rallied supporters to opposing points of view were Vicente Lombardo Toledano, a prominent labor leader increasingly holding socialist views, and Antonio Caso, probably the most noted teacher at the National University and one well known for his humanistic and moderate political values. On the surface the central debate seemed to revolve around the right to teach what one believed, but the underlying conflict resulted from differing perceptions among academic and political leadership as to the role the university should play in Mexico's development.

126

A Public Career, 1933–1939

One group, led by Antonio Caso, favored academic freedom, a position hard to dispute when you teach. But his position became a defense for keeping the university a strictly academic institution free from the expectation that they should persuade students to openly advocate certain political ideas. By contrast, opposing groups, who rallied around Lombardo Toledano, believed that if the university persisted in teaching all beliefs, it would in fact remain an elitist institution. In their view, the university preserved the status quo of future generations of political and social leaders who would simply espouse the same ideas as their predecessors. Specifically, they saw the need for the state to become supreme and for the university to train students in only certain acceptable ideologies embraced by the state. Ultimately, those who wanted to turn the university into a political classroom lost out, and Lombardo Toledano and his followers had to go outside of the university to start their own institution, the Workers' University.

Amidst this academic skirmish at the University, and as a direct result of it, my mentor Gómez Morín became rector. In turn, he relieved me of most of my duties at the law office so that I could serve as his special assistant during his rectorship. Among the tasks I performed was dealing with student representatives whose demands fell outside regular administrative channels.

One day late in 1933, a student leader from one of these groups came to see me. He asked about my knowledge of the forthcoming selection of a new law-school dean. Each of the professional schools at the National University had a dean. The rector of the university chose the deans from a *terna,* a slate of three candidates recommended by a group of professors within the professional school concerned. This student suggested that his group wished to see a Professor Carlos Sansores become the new dean.

I thanked him for the information and asked him how it

concerned me. He explained that his group wanted me to convey their preference to the rector. Although I was pleased to do that, I wanted the student to know that no slate of candidates had yet been presented to my boss. Undaunted, the student requested that should Sansores appear on the *terna*, I would explain the students' support for him to Gómez Morín. I had little trouble assuring him that I would perform this small task. After some small talk, our conversation came to an end and the student left.

I did not think much more about meeting, except to make a mental note that if this particular professor was on the list of candidates, I would tell Gómez Morín about the students' preference.

Several weeks later I met again with this student, but the situation had changed. In the interlude Gómez Morín received a slate of recommended candidates, including Professor Sansores. Naturally, as promised, I informed Gómez Morín of this student faction's interests. This fact, however, didn't need to be brought to his attention since the slate of candidates had already aroused considerable controversy between two groups supporting opposing professors. Their preferences were well known. Again, I received the student leader, who asked if I remembered our previous conversation. After assuring him that I did, he asked if I had kept my promise.

I told him I had expressed his opinion to the rector.

"Did he react favorably?"

"That's hard to say. He didn't discuss it with me."

"Oh, he doesn't ask you for your opinion?" queried the student.

"Sometimes he does, and sometimes he doesn't," I replied, truthfully.

He urged me to support his candidate and to express my opinion to Gómez Morín. On principle, I told him I couldn't do so since I didn't know Professor Sansores's merits.

"I wish you would take our word for it that he's the best candidate," continued the student, trying to persuade me. "He could help your career in the university if you help us. There are other positions of influence for people like you."

"I'm glad you think so highly of my abilities," I replied sarcastically, "but I have certain principles I must maintain."

"It would be a good principle, Professor, to look to your own interests," he advised, as if to warn me.

"I'm sure it would. A useful piece of advice," I admitted. "But my interests and principles, for the moment, are one."

"I hope you'll not regret your decision."

I assured him I hoped so too. With that, the student scraped his chair against the floor, hitting my bookshelves, as he made a slight backward movement to rise and leave. As he left I hoped that we would not meet again, and we did not; however, that was due less to luck than to the fact that his candidate lost. This was my personal initiation into the realm of political pressure. From the mid-1930s on, the university I loved increasingly came under the influence of political factions. My friends and I in the 1920s considered higher education to be the training ground for public service and political careers; however, that ideal has since been poisoned by the intervention of outside groups with sectarian political interests and by gangs of young men and women who do not belong on a university campus.

These groups have emasculated higher education. Instead of teaching young people the skills we need to govern this society, and to initiate economic growth, our most prestigious institution has permitted itself to succumb to misguided student pressures. The quality of teaching has declined, as enrollment expands. Each time a rector tries to change these conditions, the students, often with outside help, thwart his efforts. By permitting this situation to continue, we are destroying our own future, and that of Mexico. We need to recover the spirit prevailing in the 1920s and restore the university to its true mission of preparing future leaders.

18

A Winner

In 1934, the political scene changed markedly in Mexico. Ex-president Calles continued to dominate national politics. Nonetheless, it was an election year, and in those times an election produced instability, resulting largely from the unpredictability of who would be the official party candidate. My friends and I watched curiously as the infighting began. To our surprise, and for reasons not entirely clear to us, Lázaro Cárdenas, a young revolutionary from my home state, emerged at the top of the heap, becoming Calles's choice and that of the National Revolutionary Party.

Some of my colleagues at the university suggested we form a group to support Cárdenas's candidacy. Many of them were from Michoacán. I was enthusiastic. One of my former law professors, a political activist, became the director of the group; I was elected secretary. We called ourselves *El Comité Popular de Estudiantes y Profesores Pro-Cárdenas*. Since we needed more members, I took charge of a recruitment program. Relying heavily on my old contacts with the Gómez and Vasconcelos campaigns and many of my own students, I expanded our numbers considerably. One of my most helpful companions, Amado Cosío, from my preparatory days on *Eureka*, took charge of publicity.

We pooled personal donations together and ran three-column ads in *Excélsior* and *El Universal*, committing ourselves to Cárdenas and encouraging others to join in our support. My political activities increasingly brought me into arguments with my mentor Gómez Morín, who did not support Cárdenas's succession. During the years I worked for him, he became increasingly critical and cynical about Mexico's political possibilities. We argued over potential solutions, and he encouraged me to consider organizing an opposition party using ex-Vasconcelistas instead of supporting an official candidate chosen under the influence of the man we had both opposed earlier, Plutarco Calles. However, his position seemed unrealistic to me. After all, I had supported three previous candidates—Múgica, Gómez, and Vasconcelos—all of whom lost. Idealism did not appeal to me anymore. I was more mature. I wanted to support a winner. A winner—that's what Cárdenas would be.

In the 1920s, Gómez Morín had been in the mainstream of liberal, revolutionary thought. He favored a strong state, an efficient national banking system, and an effective, responsive bureaucracy. In fact, most Mexicans don't realize that he actually worked as a lawyer for the Soviet Trade Delegation to Mexico in 1928. We originally shared a political basis for our friendship because he had supported the movement led by Adolfo de la Huerta against President Obregón in 1923. Six years later we both supported Vasconcelos. But, whereas I grew disillusioned with opposing the hegemony of the post-revolutionary leadership, my mentor grew disillusioned with having been part of that leadership. He became increasingly conservative in his views, both about the role of the state and the secular supremacy of the state toward the Catholic Church.

A Public Career, 1933–1939

His critical attitudes toward the state, the political system, and the socialistic trends in education polarized in his own efforts in 1939 to found and lead the preeminent organization of the Right, the National Action Party. In my later years I came to understand his criticism of bureaucratic inefficiency and corruption, but I never really understood his reasons for sympathizing with the Church.

My beliefs toward the Church are not radical. Yet, at the time, I believed all of the provisions restricting the clergy's role in secular affairs were justified. Today, I would modify my position on some provisions, but essentially, I have no use for the argument that the Church should be allowed to re-emerge as a voice in politics. Mexico's history repeatedly illustrates the terrible consequences of such a revival. I'm a firm believer in separation of church and state and in the supremacy of civil authority. To me, Gómez Morín was toying with the revival of old conflicts that had produced long periods of dissension and civil violence.

Because of my choice, however, I lost a close friendship—with Gómez Morín. Politics was very much part of our lives. I respected him, but we no longer saw eye to eye on the major issues. I couldn't accept his views on fundamental national questions of the day or even his interpretation of nineteenth-century political history. It was a difficult choice, like leaving the father I had never had. We would remain friends, but we would never return to the easy intimacy of our earlier relationship.

One day, soon after our disagreement over my political career, the director of our group called me up. "General Cárdenas has just returned from Tamaulipas and plans to go to Michoacán for several weeks. He asked me to recommend a doctor who knows the medical problems of his home state. I told him I would ask you. Do you know someone who has a strong social consciousness?"

Part Four

"Well, yes, I think I do," I replied. "One of my classmates at the Colegio de San Nicolás, Leopoldo Vela, graduated from the National Medical School and is working on a study of leprosy with the Department of Health."

"Has he had much contact with the people," asked my professor, "or is this a desk job?"

"No," I told him, "according to a letter I received from him several months ago, Vela travels throughout Michoacán and southern Guanajuato, visiting homes and writing up individual cases. He came from a poor, working-class family."

"Wonderful, he sounds like just the person we need. The general wants someone to travel with him who has a medical background."

"He's somewhat shy," I warned, "but other than that, I think he would be ideal."

Pleased, he asked me to contact Vela, explain what Cárdenas wanted, and indicated that the general would be in Morelia the following Monday. He then asked me if I could take off from my law practice for several weeks.

"I think I can arrange it," I replied. "Why?"

"I'd like you to go to Morelia and personally introduce your friend to the general. Also, you could be useful to him on his travels to your home region. Do you think you can go?"

I told him I would try very hard to do so.

The next day I was on the train on my way to Morelia. I hadn't been back to Purépero for more than two years. My grandmother died during my second year at the Law School, but my sister Camila was well, having been married three years now, with one child and a second on the way. My mother was still teaching school, although I sent her a monthly check out of my earnings to supplement her income. Señor Romero was prospering and continued to look after my family.

I wired Leopoldo to wait for me at the Hotel Virreyes on the main square. We were supposed to meet General Cárdenas

134

there at 10:00 A.M., but I left instructions for Leopoldo to join me for breakfast. A high ceiling covered the dining room. A stairwell to the lodgings rose in the back of the main floor. Beige pillars of cement, polished through years of dusting, stood like stone sentinels around the outer edges. Because of the wide overhang of the exterior arcade, even in the morning the interior remained gloomy and the electric chandeliers glowed.

I found Leopoldo sitting at a table near the main desk. He had put on weight since we last met. His hair had receded nearly a third of the way back on his head. Glasses gave his rotund face a more serious facade. The suit he wore was plain, reflecting the simple tastes of its owner. His nervous hands, grasping and clenching a cup, revealed the boundless energy inside a body and face that were outwardly calm. As my shadow crossed his table, he looked up.

"How great to see you," he said, as he grasped me in a long, back-pounding *abrazo*. "How's life in the capital?"

"Busy, as usual. What about you?"

"Ah, there's always too much to do here. But my work progresses."

I asked him what he had been doing.

"Well, as I wrote in my last letter, I'm studying a number of leprosy cases in this region. It's much more widespread than I had imagined before embarking on this project," he explained, sadly shaking his head.

"It's because we have never had enough doctors to treat the people here."

"That's true, Toño, but I've reached the conclusion that preventive health care will be more successful than the curing skills of physicians. It means," he went on, "that you spend more time on the educational aspects to prevent disease, rather than the less satisfactory, more costly approach of trying to identify and cure a disease once it has attacked the body. It takes too long to train a doctor, and besides, most doctors will

135

not return to the provinces. We can train teachers more quickly. If we make education focus on personal and family hygiene in collaboration with health measures provided for and enforced by the government, these diseases will be reduced."

"Sounds reasonable to me."

"It is, Toño. Not only reasonable, but right. We need to persuade some doctors to give up private practice to help us achieve these goals. We also need to convince the government to put more funds into preventive programs, rather than research related to cures. The cures will come, but now we can help more people using the first approach."

"Maybe you can persuade General Cárdenas about your concerns?"

"I was sort of hoping to have the opportunity. That's the main reason I'm willing to spend the time with him. I'm not a politician," he admitted. "Politics make me uncomfortable." Leopoldo was unique among my political friends. He was always frank. It was refreshing to speak to him. He never hid anything from his friends. This quality made him fun to tease.

"Do I make you uncomfortable, Leopoldo?" I asked seriously, with underlying humor.

"Huh, of, of course not . . . you're crazy," he replied, embarrassed at belatedly catching my meaning.

"I'm a politician of sorts," I joked.

He laughed. "Yes, that's true. It's not the people, it's the profession."

When I asked him what he meant, he offered a rather insightful analysis of my future career.

"Politics, like medicine, has its own culture. But one of the special qualities of politics is to be adept at achieving what you want in exchange for something the other fellow can't have. At least, that's how I perceive it. So it seems to me that you have to perfect your skills at deceiving your colleagues as to your precise intentions. Otherwise, you never obtain what you want. Yet, I like men who shoot straight from the hip. It's too hard to try and figure out what's meant from what's said, and is it for real this time. Truthfully, I don't have the patience for it. I want to know what's going on in real life, not just play acting."

"The play acting may be the real activity."

We heard a commotion outside. Men's voices broke the silence around us. A group stepped through the door, their identities unknown to us as we stared blindly into the light above their heads. They passed into the interior, and the central figure, upright and slightly stiff, turned toward our table. It was Cárdenas. The gloom did not return to the room. Mexico's political future was here. Would we be part of it?

19

Election
Times Three

The skin was soft. His hair was unusually wavy for a Mexican, and the hairline receded on the sides. As was the custom of the time, his sideburns were short and cropped high on his earlobe, almost in military fashion. The protrusion of the upper lip was exaggerated by a short, bushy mustache extending to the end of the mouth. A weakness of the lower jaw and chin were visible only from a profile. He wore a well-used cardigan sweater, a white shirt and checkered tie, and carried a light-colored stetson in his left hand. He looked exactly like his pictures. His eyes were quiet, his stare somber, but an inner warmth shone through the facial features.

General Cárdenas was always surrounded by a circle of admirers or mere sycophants; but while people were drawn to him, there was always a space, as though a magnetic field separated him from them wherever he went. After exchanging remarks with several people, he graciously broke away, accompanied by one of his Michoacán campaign leaders, a man I'd met previously in Mexico City. They drew near our table and Leopoldo and I stood up. I greeted my acquaintance, who introduced me to Cárdenas. Cárdenas clasped his left hand around my right in a firm grip. I then introduced him to Leopoldo, to whom he was equally warm and gracious.

The man who introduced us excused himself to arrange some other matters. We sat down and ordered coffee. The general laid his hat on the table and began to ask Leopoldo some questions.

"I have been traveling throughout Mexico, Dr. Vela. The depth of our health and educational problems can be discouraging, but I'm optimistic that our government can do something about these problems. In many parts of Mexico, in the North, the South, and the West, I've found individuals like you who are willing to help cope with rural development. Many of us fought in the Revolution for social change—the masses still need to benefit from that Revolution. How do you see the medical problems fitting into such a new order?"

"It's a very complex situation, General. Perhaps the most obvious aspect of this situation is the lack of medically trained people in rural areas, a condition you're probably very much aware of."

Cárdenas nodded, encouraging Leopoldo to continue.

"I wish we could increase the number of physicians in the countryside, but I doubt that is possible," replied Leopoldo discouragingly.

Cárdenas asked if expanding the medical schools would help this situation. But according to Leopoldo, the National Medical School professors, on the whole, didn't encourage their students to go into the public service. As a consequence, he explained, most graduates pursued private careers in Mexico City or the most prosperous cities of their home states. Leopoldo concluded that what was being taught, and for what purpose, were more important to improving general health than the size of medical student enrollment.

The General also wanted to know how the government's resources could best be spent.

Leopoldo quickly replied. "One direction we might pursue is to increase the rural population's education, not just formally, but in personal hygiene. This would be a more direct way, I believe, of attacking the problem."

"Doctor, that's a good approach," agreed Cárdenas. "What else do you recommend?"

"I think we need greater emphasis on those public-health programs that attempt to understand diseases prevalent in rural, undeveloped regions. Because the best people stay in the cities, they, and the universities, concentrate on incurable diseases which don't attack most rural people. For example, heart disease. The average peasant doesn't live long enough to die of a heart attack. It's usually a tropical disease like malaria, or more seriously, intestinal and stomach disorders. In addition to these, malnutrition and inadequate sanitation are rampant."

Cárdenas seemed to be making a mental note of these suggestions. I thought Leopoldo really had captured his attention, and I became the interested observer. He wanted to know what his government could do to stress public health.

"Of course I don't have much experience in administrative matters," suggested Leopoldo, "and to be frank, General, I'm allergic to politics. But, I think allocating more funds to the Health Department to promote the expansion of this program and to recruit doctors at better pay, so that they will choose public-health careers, would help. Also, we could decentralize our facilities away from Mexico City and create an institute or two at the provincial level to do research on those diseases prevalent in the areas that I mentioned earlier."

"For a person aloof from politics, doctor, you have some very practical ideas. Do you have other suggestions to accomplish your goals?"

With his usual frankness, Leopoldo told the General, "I'm sure I could talk on this until I would bore you. Perhaps it would be better if I saved my other ideas for another time."

"Doctor, you would have to go much farther before I would tire of listening to you. But, as you wish. We will be seeing a lot of each other in the next few weeks. I would like to visit some villages with you where these conditions are most common. Can we start at 6:00 A.M. on Thursday?"

Leopoldo agreed enthusiastically. Cárdenas explained that an assistant would call to finalize the plans.

Cárdenas turned toward me and asked me to stay a few minutes. Leopoldo excused himself and left.

"*Licenciado*, thank you for your patience in listening to our conversation. But I wanted to speak with you, too. I understand you're a native of Michoacán from the Purépero region?"

"Yes, General, I grew up in Purépero."

"Well, I'd like to visit there and would appreciate your company on my trip. Can you stay a few days?"

"I would be delighted, General, since it would allow me to visit my family."

"Fine, then, you can leave tomorrow?"

"Yes," I replied, "whenever you like."

"Good, we will depart from here just before sunrise."

The next day we left the hotel in a battered, dust-covered black touring car. A driver and an aide occupied the front seat; General Cárdenas and I shared the back seat. We travelled part way by automobile, and the rest of our trip on horseback. I felt awkward at first, wondering what I would talk about with the future president of Mexico. But my fears were unfounded; Cárdenas was interested in me personally and my views on a wide range of Mexican problems. He readily explored these with me as we jolted and bumped down the highway. After talking about my background and discussing some of my political experiences, he turned to my perceptions of the future.

"As a lawyer, my young friend, what do you feel is necessary for Mexico's future?"

"Because of my profession I'm biased in my perception of the importance of the law. Keeping this in mind, General, I've reached the conclusion that law must play a social role in the development of our society. My best professors stressed the opportunities for the creation of new laws to guide Mexico after the Revolution. I can now see they were men of vision. Structurally, many areas have begun to change, for example, new legislation in agrarian questions and more recently in labor law. Of course I welcome these expanded professional opportunities, but I think the law should take a more active role."

"In what sense?" interrupted Cárdenas.

"Well, my thoughts are similar to Leopoldo's. The state should use the law to alter our society's economic and social backwardness. I want to see the government apply laws for social purposes. Many of my professors and some of my colleagues wouldn't agree, but I don't think that the law in our society can be an objective, neutral force. It has to be directed to the positive support of political and social reforms."

"An interesting idea, *Licenciado*. And if you had the opportunity, how would you go about using law for social purposes, as you call it, within the government?"

"I'm not really sure. I'm interested in the study of economics, and I think that certain economic policies, if legislated, might bring about some of the changes I believe Mexico needs."

The General nodded understandingly. "Do you have some in mind?"

"I have been thinking about some of the programs North Americans are using since President Roosevelt was elected.

144

Because the Mexican situation is so obviously different from that of our northern neighbor, I would like to see us do more to promote industrial growth so we could become independent economically and employ peasants from the rural sector. Also, we need a clearer agrarian reform program. Lastly, some day I hope we can use taxes as a means to redistribute the wealth in Mexico."

"You have some very progressive ideas." He tapped me on the sleeve. "Perhaps you will have an opportunity to realize some of them."

I told him I hoped I would.

20

Private Practice, Public Business

Cárdenas was elected President. He took office in 1934 and appointed a new cabinet, some of whom were holdovers from the Calles era. Among those who became part of his select group was Francisco Múgica, who took charge of the Ministry of Economy. Múgica once again became a figure of national importance. Many old friends from our campaign days came to live in Mexico City. There were also new employees in the Ministry of Economy. Like every other Mexican political figure, Múgica long had been building up an *equipo*, a group or team who had remained loyal to him, hoping to improve their chances for successful bureaucratic careers. Now they would cash in and assume positions around their leader. Other Mugicistas who didn't work in the ministry came to Mexico, among them Andrés Bustamante, who had been elected deputy from Michoacán just before Cárdenas took office. That event made possible the renewal of our old friendship.

Late in the year I opened a small law office on Juárez Street. Amado Cosío joined me and we struggled to make ends meet. Andrés gave our firm an unexpected boost after inviting me to

147

lunch at the Café Tacuba. As usual we talked politics, but then, pushing away a partly eaten plate of chili rellenos and ordering coffee, he introduced a new theme in our conversation.

"Toño, I was wondering if you and Amado would be interested in a new partner?"

"A new partner? I wish we were doing well enough to have a dozen new associates. I'm afraid things aren't going well. Why, who did you have in mind?"

"Me," he said, pointing to his chest.

"You!" I responded, surprised. "But with your influential position as a deputy, why would you be interested in participating in our struggling firm?"

"That's just it. With my position and my contacts in Michoacán, I think we could establish a successful firm in Mexico City. The central government is everything, Toño. People in the provinces who want to go places are dealing increasingly with government agencies. To do that, they have to come to Mexico City since very few branch offices exist elsewhere. And even if such offices did exist, there would still be that certain individual to see somewhere high up in the national bureaucracy."

I nodded in agreement.

"With Múgica in the cabinet, we both have access to officials in the public-works sector. This is a lucrative area for government contracts. It's too expensive for people to travel to and from Mexico City, facing delays, and lacking the right contacts. Together, we can make these contacts. I can't be your formal partner, expressed on the sign across your doorway, because I'm not a lawyer. But if you turn your partnership into a company, we could each hold equal shares. My contribution would be to increase business for all of us."

"It sounds like a good proposal, Andrés. Perhaps you're right. Maybe we are competing for only those city residents who need legal help and could do better with those living out-side Mexico City."

"I'm convinced it's true. Think about my offer."

I assured him I would let him know after I had talked to Amado. We had some dessert, talked further, and went back to our separate offices.

Andrés had changed since we had worked for Múgica to-gether in Michoacán. I never thought he was interested in money. His social ideas always dominated everything else. Maybe he was looking to the future. He wouldn't always be a federal deputy, especially since by then the Constitution pro-hibited an individual from serving consecutive terms. I won-dered if perhaps age made you more realistic and less roman-tic about the future. After all, being progressive doesn't mean you have to be poor; and there was nothing dishonest about his suggestion. Things were accomplished through friend-ships. It was a good idea, whatever his personal motivations. I talked to Amado. He needed little persuasion. Immediately he saw the possibilities and agreed we should let Andrés in.

In the next year our business improved by leaps and bounds. Whereas before it had seemed as though we had only part-time jobs, we worked more and more in the evenings. Our secretary went from half a day to a full workweek, and my time as a professor at the National University became increas-ingly restricted. The government was like an ancient Aztec god—it could shower you with its benefits or stymie your achievements. As our legal demands increased, so did our successes.

One of our more interesting clients during this busy period made his entrance late one afternoon in July. My buzzer rang. The secretary announced that a gentleman, a Señor Contreras, wished to see me about a legal problem. I told her to show him in. Removing my feet from my desk top, I swiveled my chair toward the entrance. A pudgy, middle-aged man stepped in. He wore a white shirt, with no tie, and the collar was frayed and discolored. Beads of sweat gathered on his forehead and the sides and back of his neck. He held a crumpled handkerchief in his left hand, which he used ineffectively to swipe at the moisture on his face. After rubbing his palms with this damp ball of material, he extended his hand to me in greeting. I asked him how I could assist him.

"Well, *Licenciado*, I represent Cementos Michoacanos, S.A., a firm doing business in the state of Michoacán. Romero, your *compadre*, suggested that you might be of some use to our firm."

Surprised, I said, "You know Romero?"

"Yes, he has some business dealings with my boss. A good man, your *compadre*."

I asked him to continue.

"The governor has succeeded in persuading the federal government to improve the state highways. We, of course, are most interested in obtaining some of the paving contracts for our firm." The man paused, his fat hand fidgeting with the front of his shirt which hung out over his belt, twisted and strained from the pressure of his bulging stomach.

"I understand," I nodded. "Do you need legal services?"

"Not exactly, *Licenciado*, we need you to represent us in the acquisition of these contracts."

I asked if he had an office in Mexico City.

"No, we don't have enough business here to be able to afford the luxury of our own representative."

"Well, what did you have in mind?" I inquired.

"I understand you know people in the Ministry of Public Works."

I told him this was true and asked if he was having some difficulty with their contracts with the ministry.

"No, not really," he explained, "we haven't been very successful in obtaining federal contracts since the new state gov-

150

ernor came in. We thought that by hiring your firm to represent us before the ministry, you might use your contacts to help us obtain contracts."

"Actually, Señor Contreras, we don't really represent firms in this manner, in the sense of initiating contracts. Normally, we handle the legal arrangements of contracts already reached between the government and private parties."

Undaunted, Contreras continued. "Yes, yes, I understand, *Licenciado*. But it's very difficult to get those contracts without knowing the right people. Of course, we want you to be our legal agent, but first we need to get some contracts for you to handle. The more contracts we obtain with the ministry, the more legal business we can give you. That's beneficial to both of us, and of course, it helps our home state." He followed this with a personal question. "You are from Michoacán, no?"

"I'm a native," I replied.

"Well, the large firms from Monterrey are taking all of the business in our home state from the federal government. We need to stick together to help each other."

"I understand, but the contracts for roads are usually obtained through bids."

"Yes and no," he explained. "These aren't always public. And besides, a word from the right person might get them to give us favorable attention. What we want your firm to do is to put in a word for us. We'll inform you in advance of the contracts we're interested in. We'll pay you consulting fees for each attempt, and a bonus if we get the contract. All legal fees involving each contract will be given to your firm."

"I can't make any promises, Señor Contreras, but I like your proposition. Let me say that I'll try this arrangement for a year and see if we have some success. Is that agreeable?"

"Very much so, *Licenciado*. My partners will be most elated with your decision."

"Fine, I'll have my secretary draw up an agreement

151

to serve as your agent under the terms stipulated."

He thanked me and I asked him to remember me to Señor Romero. As he left, he said he was sure this would be the beginning of a long relationship.

Contreras's prediction was fulfilled. Cementos Michoacanos, S.A. grew rapidly, becoming the largest contracting firm in Michoacán and the surrounding region as well as the best of clients. It's not what you might think. Bribery wasn't involved. I don't remember the particulars about how we got our first contract for Cementos Michoacanos because Andrés handled the contacts with the ministry. But I'm sure the person in charge found some need for a favor from a cement company for someone in his circle, or a friend or family member back in our native state. This is our way of life. Politics is no exception. Once you ensure those contacts, and cultivate them carefully, they multiply.

The personal contacts we had developed for Cementos Michoacanos, S.A. were forerunners of those we acquired over the years for many other clients. The fine points of law weren't a key to our success, they only complemented our assets in personal contacts, making contractual relationships among businesses and between government and business possible. And, sometimes relationships would not be all business.

21

A
Domestic Interlude

The remainder of the 1930s found me increasingly successful and prosperous as a lawyer. With some of the money from my firm's profits I began to invest in real estate. San Angel, a wooded, colonial suburb of downtown Mexico City, was one of the places where land was still cheap. After much searching, I purchased a huge lot on which was a two-story home, several hundred years old, which had fallen into disrepair. I hired a contractor and, over a period of two years, restored it to its original grandeur.

It was during this time that material goods became more attractive to me. I began acquiring antiques and artifacts to furnish the walls and floors of my home. I especially prized the library, two stories high with floor to ceiling bookcases. A balcony ran along the bottom of the second floor, and since the ceilings were high, I hired a carpenter to construct two ladders attached at their upper extremities to a rail running along the edge of the top shelf. Using this system, I could more easily retrieve works above my reach.

The walls of the house were nearly a foot thick, and that

fact, combined with the smallness of the windows and the shade of centuries old trees, made the interior seem cool and dark the year round. And although I had the walls painted an off-white, each room and the windows were framed in hand-carved walnut, which did little to reflect the light. As time went by, with the acquisition of more furnishings, my home took on added warmth.

As a man of means I could now invite my mother to come to Mexico City to live with me. She was reluctant to leave her friends and my sister but, with the approach of old age, she was attracted to the idea of running my home. With only enough belongings to fill one large trunk, she arrived in Mexico City as I had some fifteen years earlier. Although she was unable to fully master the ways of dealing with servants with whom she had more in common than with the *señoras* of other city homes, she adjusted well to the environment.

My comfortable financial status also improved my social life, as I took more time to relax and to entertain at home. Many of my friends, married in their late twenties, continued their luncheon engagements with me, but found less and less to do in the evenings with a bachelor friend. Their few spare hours were consumed by family responsibilities. My single-minded goal of success had left me with little time for a serious affair with someone of the opposite sex, except for the flirtations I had as a student. So I began, as the gringos say, to make up for lost time.

In the fall of 1939, while attending the opening of a show for Juan O'Gorman, Amado introduced me to a young woman named Emma Sepúlveda. Her father was a prominent scientist, an expert in mathematics. Her mother, a North American descendant of a Southern general in the American Civil War, married her father after meeting him at Harvard, where he had earned his Ph.D. The entire family resided in Mexico City, where Dr. Sepúlveda taught at the National University and served as a consultant to several engineering firms.

Emma was a striking young woman, even in the midst of the cream of Mexican society. Her dual heritage gave her a light complexion, hazel eyes, the fine, high cheekbones of the Indian, and unusual auburn hair. Her lashes, darker than her hair, were long and slender, accentuating the femininity of her face. She wore a blue silk dress, with a white embroidered trim around the oval neckline. Blue, star-sapphire pendant earrings and a matching necklace were her only jewelry. When we were introduced, she was twenty years old, a student of philosophy at the School of Arts and Letters. After the usual social amenities, I invited her to sit down and talk. Her conversation revealed a well-read and inquisitive mind to match her superior beauty.

The following month we met again, this time at a party given by a mutual friend. Before departing I invited her to go to a concert at Bellas Artes the following week. When that evening arrived, I picked her up in a taxi at her home in Coyoacán, another colonial section in Mexico City not far from where the Diego Rivera and Frida Kahlo home is now located. It was a fairly long trip by car, and we talked animatedly about many subjects, arriving early for the performance. I purchased choice seats for the concert to impress my date. They were in the front, ground-floor section of Bellas Artes, but I always had had a romantic attachment to the balcony seats from my frugal days as a student. From the third-floor section, because of the steep angle of the descent, one immediately gains a sense of the massiveness of the building, including an eerie, almost gravitational pull toward its center. Perhaps because it was the first place Emma and I found ourselves alone together, I continue to be attracted by its classic yet somewhat ugly mixture of architectural designs.

155

Part Four

After the concert, which was mediocre at best, we went to Sanborns's House of Tiles, continuing our conversation over coffee and sweets. Remembering to keep my promise to her mother not to stay out late, I dropped her off at home and returned to my own residence in San Angel. We began to see each other regularly during the next six months and, in the late spring, I asked her to marry me. The wedding was set for mid-summer and was a gala affair. My Catholicism was an unpracticed, vague belief, but after obtaining our civil license, we had a large, church wedding. A mixture of my social and political friends were there, most prominent of whom was Múgica. His presence, and the stature of Dr. Sepúlveda, guaranteed us widespread coverage in the society section of *Excélsior* the following day.

We traveled to San Francisco for our honeymoon. For me, it was the first opportunity to practice my school-learned English; but Emma, who was bilingual, felt entirely at home. We stayed at the Mark Hopkins Hotel, where we spent two evenings dancing at the Top of the Mark to the same North American rhythms then popular in Mexico City. While sightseeing at the usual tourist attractions, we spent most of our money buying clothes and gifts for each other, as well as for our families.

In November of 1939, four months after we were married, Emma was pregnant with our first child and soon dropped out of the university. My daily routine changed, too. I no longer stayed downtown for lunch, but came home for the afternoon meal with my wife and mother. By spring, we had settled into this as a regular pattern. Perhaps my life would have proved prosperous but uneventful, if this schedule continued. One doesn't know. But this was not to be the case.

I received a call from an aide to Agustín Leñero, Private Secretary to President Cárdenas, asking me to call Leñero. I did so, and he indicated that the President would like to see me. It had been more than five years since our conversation in Morelia, to which I had given little thought in the last few years. When I asked him why the President wished to see me, he replied, "I do not know, *Licenciado*, but you can rest assured it's important."

I could not disagree with his answer and found myself with an appointment the next day. With some trepidation, I waited for the hour of our meeting to arrive. I took a taxi to the National Palace and, arriving early, was led to an anteroom. The trappings of the office forced the knot in my stomach to tighten and the rumbling from my intestines to become unbearably loud. Finally, the President's secretary came to the door, and showed me into his office.

Cárdenas obviously had aged from the rigors of office, but his appearance seemed remarkably like what I remembered from our first encounter. Except for somewhat haggard features, he looked unchanged. As I entered, he rose quickly to his feet, came around his desk, and grasped me in an *abrazo*, greeting me warmly.

"Ay, my young lawyer, it has been too long!" he said cheerfully.

"Yes, *Señor Presidente*. Your office seems to have agreed well with you."

"Ah, yes, it has its ups and downs. And how are you? I understand you're expecting a child?"

"Yes, Mr. President, this summer," I replied, barely keeping the surprised look off my face. It amazed me that he would've known so much about my personal life.

"That's good news, Antonio, congratulations. Please sit down, my friend, I have something I want to tell you."

We relaxed on a comfortable, but well-used couch. "You know, Antonio, we'll soon be in the midst of a congressional election."

"Yes," I replied.

"Well, we need qualified candidates to represent the party

in many districts, including your home district in Michoacán. I want you to serve Mexico and become the candidate from Zamora. Are you interested?"

I reacted with a loss of words and I felt my face redden as my cheeks warmed up. "Why, I don't know, *Señor Presidente*, I mean . . . well, this is so sudden."

"Yes, of course," he nodded understandingly, "I have taken you by surprise, but you don't need to give me an answer right now. Next week is fine, before I talk to the party leaders."

I thanked him for asking me, explaining that I considered it an honor.

"I don't forget able people, Antonio, my memory is long," he said, patting my arm.

In those days, young men interested in politics didn't always immediately embark upon a government career, the way most politically ambitious students do today. Oftentimes, they practiced their profession before immersing themselves in the political world. It seems today the professional politician has taken over, but I remain unconvinced that they have managed affairs better than we. After Vasconcelos's fiasco, I was very disillusioned with politics. I even considered remaining aloof. But power is a persistent lure. There's an inherently exciting quality about public life so that once you taste it, it becomes addictive.

22

A Return
to Politics

The answer was yes. I would be a candidate of the Mexican Revolutionary Party. I filed my candidacy and, several weeks later, left for Michoacán. In Morelia, there was more bustle than the last time I visited, but the downtown sections remained largely unchanged. My first stop was the PRM headquarters to meet with the state director of the party. I found it in a shabbily furnished office on a side street off the main square. Its walls were plastered with uneven political posters. Leaning against them were several delegations of peasants waiting to see the party head. Inside, the room reeked of sweat and the sweet smell of Mexican tobacco.

A young man wearing a rumpled suit and a jersey shirt buttoned at the neck sat at a battered desk covered with papers overflowing into two dilapidated cartons on the floor. Nervously he jabbed the butt of a cigarette into a black dish, glancing in my direction. I introduced myself and he swiftly got up, pulled out a straight-back chair for me, and then disappeared through a rear door. Moments later he returned and ushered me into another office. It was somewhat neater, with a cabinet

159

along one wall, pictures of Cárdenas and Madero staring down from the other, and a desk in the middle. The face of the man behind the desk was familiar, one which I hesitated only momentarily in placing.

"Germán," I cried with surprise, "it's you?"

"Toño, you didn't know it was me, huh," he said laughing. "We lost track of you, too. But Leopoldo has kept me up-to-date on you professionally, even if erratically. Let's sit down and talk about your campaign." He motioned me to an armchair.

"I would like that," I said, clasping my hands together. "I'm out of touch with my state. What's happening?"

"Well, the situation is in flux here because of Governor Magaña's early attempts as a precandidate against Avila Camacho, and his unexpected death last December. That means, of course, that candidates aren't being pushed by the interim governor since he has little strength. Of course, General Cárdenas keeps a tight reign on his home state, but our local leadership is slightly disorganized. You're lucky, though. National headquarters will pay closer attention to you," he added, motioning his right hand toward me.

"Why's that, Germán?" I asked, surprised.

Germán sat back in his chair, relaxed. "The General Delegate of the party is a close friend of Cárdenas's, so I'm sure you will receive preferential treatment from him during the campaign. That translates into more campaign funds and appearances from prominent party leaders."

"That will be helpful. What about my opposition?"

"Hmmm. . . . Frankly, I think you have a good situation," he smiled. "The filing date has passed and the new Panista party hasn't registered a candidate.

Secretly I was relieved to hear that since, as I mentioned earlier, the party's major founder was my old mentor Manuel Gómez Morín. I didn't want to oppose him, if only indirectly, by running against a candidate from his party. He had by 1939 become an avowed anti-Cárdenista. Gathering up some of the people from the antireelectionist days of Madero and from the 1929 Vasconcelos campaign, and with the help of his influential friends from academia and the private sector, Gómez Morín organized this new party. It was so proclerical I was embarrassed for him.

From a historical perspective, I could understand how his party had come about. Cárdenas didn't help to mollify the Catholic Church after Calles had so bluntly confronted its authority. Portes Gil had skillfully settled the Cristero rebellion in 1929, but Cárdenas revived the conflict between church and state over education early in his administration. The ideas of socialist education, which had been hotly debated at the National University in the early 1930s, created more furor in the provinces where many government-appointed schoolteachers became the victims of angry peasants. Fortunately, Cárdenas had eased off the pressure on the Church, and instead of giving the presidential nod to Múgica, who would have followed the same path, Cárdenas chose a moderate, General Avila Camacho, as his successor. My Múgica friends felt sold out. Cárdenas, I believe, did what was best for Mexico.

In the years immediately after the Revolution, during the formation of our national party, government leaders were a heterogeneous group. Now, I'm not suggesting that isn't true today; but by comparison, the extremes were more exaggerated then, and the consequences more obvious. I remember one of my friends showing me the calling card of the secretary of agriculture's chief executive officer, who in addition to listing such pertinent occupational information as congressman and member of our party, added "Personal Enemy of God" in black, embossed letters. These radicals, or some might call them purists, wanted to enforce every provision of the Constitution to its extreme. No compromise existed for these true believers. Fortunately, although the party's scope is broad, we gradually have pushed the extremists, both radical and conservative, from our midst. They can now find their expression in the smaller, opposition parties. But let me return to my conversation with Germán Torres.

"So that leaves me with just one competitor," I replied.

"Yes, *hombre*, the Prunista. That turncoat Almazán and his bastards!" he shouted, angrily pounding his desk with his fist.

Germán was referring to the newly formed personalist party of General Almazán, who had resigned from the Army to oppose the PRM candidate under his own party banner, PRUN, the Revolutionary Party of National Unification. Germán's disgust with Almazán rose from the general having originally been a Maderista, then a supporter of the reactionary General Huerta, after which he reverted to the Constitutionalists. For many Mexicans he could never live down that political mistake. After all, you were either a revolutionary or reactionary, but you couldn't be both.

"What's my opponent like?"

"He's a physician from Zamora," replied Germán evenly, having regained his composure.

"How's his support?"

"Well, to tell the truth, he's got considerable appeal among professional groups and businessmen. Many haven't been too pleased with Magaña's administration. Of course the clergy will support him. They have little good to say about Cárdenas, but their influence is insignificant. Actually, the man isn't a bad fellow. He's honest. He has organized several committees for better government in Zamora. Also, he helped start a clinic to improve health care services in the city."

"Ay, *hombre*," I sighed, "he sounds damn strong to me."

"No, no, Toño, not really," mused Germán.

"But from your description. . . ."

"That's just the good part for him—and bad for you. But, his strength is localized in Zamora. You've got a natural base in Purépero. You're a native son, remember?"

"Yes, Germán, but so is he."

"True, but his father was a doctor. You're a son of the working class. They will support you, along with the peasants. Don't worry, we will work the villages and the rural areas; we can lose the professional groups if need be. We have hundreds of loyalists in the villages and the barrios. Each one of them is campaigning for you. They know how to get their friends out to support you. We help people here and there. Lots of small favors over the years. They don't forget that when the election rolls around." Germán waxed enthusiastic as he lectured me.

"Your confidence is encouraging. What should we do first?"

"First we work out a schedule of your appearances. The local party leaders will take care of details. Also, we want to get some coverage in the Morelia papers. We have funds for advertising. I'll handle your arrangements personally, Toño, and let my aides take care of the other deputies."

"Thank you, Germán, it is a great relief to have you working for me."

"My pleasure, *hombre*. I've arranged an important engagement for you in the Zamora theater next Tuesday to kick off your campaign. Local peasant federations and labor union groups will be there. You need to prepare a speech with your principles, but, of course, talk mostly about what the Party has done and will do for the popular classes. That will take place about 8:00 P.M., and you can visit several of the villages near Zamora earlier in the afternoon."

"Sounds fine. Do we need anything else?" I queried.

"Yes, extra transportation would be helpful. Do you have any friends here who could loan you a truck?"

"Hmm, I'm not sure. Yes, I might know someone. I'll check into it." I made a note to remind myself.

Part Four

The campaign was frantic. I didn't have time to think about my family. The crowds that gathered at my talks either seemed overly boisterous or bored—but, as Germán promised, they were large. These engagements were too impersonal for me. I thought of myself as only an adequate speaker before large groups. I favored those times during the campaign when I could speak to individual party leaders and small groups of supporters in villages or district campaign headquarters. Through these experiences I got to know more clearly the people's complaints and the government's shortcomings.

General Almazán's campaign stimulated much interest in the elections. To minimize advertisements for Almazán's presidential aspirations and those of my opponent, Germán paid for numerous *gacetillas,* articles about me and my campaign, that appeared in addition to general news items. One of the unfortunate qualities about our newspapers is their unprofessional behavior. Not only can politicians buy articles to promote career aspirations but under the right circumstances, they can ensure coverage in media favorable to their cause.

During the campaign, my greatest help came from Cementos Michoacanos, S.A., which, after-hours and on weekends, loaned me several trucks to transport my supporters to various meeting places. They didn't charge a cent for the drivers or vehicles. I found that I had numerous ties to individuals and organizations, some extending back fifteen years. Old acquaintances were pleased to help me, even friends of friends. After all, I might be useful to them in Mexico City. The crowds' enthusiasm didn't increase, but attendance did.

The help of businesses and friends was crucial to the success of my campaign. Of course the party spends a lot more now than then, but people don't really understand that the party provides only a limited amount of funds for each candidate. Most of what we get are favors, which of course substitute for scarce monies. An individual candidate can spend

164

his own personal funds on his campaign, but most of us had limited resources. Consequently, the more friends we have, the more lively our campaign.

Toward the end of my campaign I began reading newspaper accounts describing disruptions at my opponent's rallies. When I asked Germán about these, he shrugged them off, saying that over-zealous party members or unruly juveniles were involved, something common to all local campaigns. I hadn't given it much further thought until one day, while resting in my hotel room, I received a telephone call.

"This is Dr. Rivera."

"Dr. Rivera? Pardon, who?" I replied, not recognizing the voice.

"Francisco Rivera, your opponent . . ."

"Of course, Dr. Rivera," I said, taken aback, "You took me by surprise. How may I help you?" I asked, regaining my composure.

"Please let me apologize in advance for disturbing you, but your *compadre*, Leopoldo Vela, whom I know professionally, suggested I call you. He said you were a fair person and would listen to my complaints."

"Yes," I paused, "well, I think of myself as just," I admitted. "What is it I could help you with?"

"If you believe in fair elections, sir, I would appreciate your intervention among your supporters. They're repeatedly disrupting my campaign. I haven't been able to hold a single gathering without catcalls, fistfights, police harrassment, and even last-minute cancellations of permits for public gatherings. Vela says you don't believe in this. Could you try to stop it? I'm becoming convinced that we Mexicans are too ignorant and undisciplined to have a democracy. You can help educate against that ignorance. I've tried everything," he concluded dejectedly.

I nodded to myself in agreement. "Of course I understand your complaint, Doctor. Leopoldo's right, I personally don't advocate this type of behavior, and I promise I will speak to my manager."

"You will, *Licenciado?* You are most gracious," he replied in a relieved voice.

"My word of honor, doctor. I hope this will end it."

"Thank you, *Licenciado,* you are a gentleman."

I thanked him and hung up the phone.

I spoke to Germán the next morning, as promised. He was pessimistic, but I insisted. The disruptions tapered off over the next few weeks. But in the final weeks of the campaign, they again became frequent, and twice my own public gatherings saw some crowd violence.

I learned two lessons from my congressional campaign. In the first place, you're not always in control of your supporters. I always had blamed Carranza for Múgica's problems in Michoacán in 1917. But, in all likelihood local leaders instigated their own techniques in support of Ortiz Rubio and in opposition to Múgica. I understood that after my own efforts. I also realized that we hadn't learned to respect our opponents' ideas. Only one person's views were correct. We claimed we wanted democracy, indeed we were ready for it. Why couldn't we compromise? We didn't have to believe in another Mexican's ideology. But we could respect his right to campaign for that idea.

Maybe my opponent was right, maybe we weren't ready for democracy. Did I have the power to change it? As a student I had thought we could. Now, in my own small realm, I could see more readily the pragmatic difficulties of a youth's ideals. Doubts began to creep in. Where would they lead me?

Part Five

Ascent and Descent
1940 – 1970

23

A Congressman

Almazán lost. So did Dr. Rivera. According to the ballots, I won eighty-seven percent of the vote in my district, receiving the highest margin of any of the PRM deputies from Michoacán. I was elated. Emma and I celebrated at the Normandie, and our small dinner party turned into a social cocktail hour as we greeted new and old friends who also were dining there. My absence from Mexico City had been a long one, and our time together before the beginning of the new sessions in September was short. During the campaign, Emma had given birth to a baby girl, whom we named María, after Emma's favorite aunt.

In late August, I received a phone call from the newly designated president of the Gran Comisión, the leader of the Chamber of Deputies. Each state is represented on this committee by the head of the state delegation to the Chamber. Usually delegation leadership went to the senior deputy from the state, generally meaning a person who had served in a previous legislature. In Michoacán in 1940, I was one of eleven deputies, and although one individual from a bordering district had served in the 1934 legislature, I became the delegation leader.

My new office near Donceles, where the Chamber stood, brought me back to my student haunts. Normally, I went there only in the afternoons, and continued to spend mornings in my law office. My first year as member of the Second Labor and First Constitutional Affairs Committees was uneventful, but I did expand my circle of friends, and we began a weekly luncheon meeting at the Del Prado, a tradition which continued for years. The group included three other congressmen, a senator, and several colleagues from the federal bureaucracy. In 1942, however, my involvement in congressional affairs increased after President Avila Camacho came to the Congress with a request for a declaration of war against the Axis. Once Mexico allied itself with the United States, cooperative arrangements and treaties multiplied. The Ministry of Government, then directed by Miguel Alemán, requested someone to represent the Chamber on a committee to make recommendations for an arrangement between the United States and Mexico for a wartime labor exchange. The majority leader asked me to serve, noting my facility with English and my previous labor experience. Our committee met regularly, and since this was a pressing matter we worked hard to make our recommendations quickly. Some members of the committee found it distasteful to be allied with the United States, and to help that country by providing them with Mexican labor.

I sympathized with their objections, but I believed that in the long run the livelihood of many individual Mexican workers and our economy as a whole would benefit from the influx of money paid out in North American salaries. Ultimately, the group agreed to recommend such a program provided there were strict safeguards for the protection of Mexican workers. In 1943, Avila Camacho and President Franklin D. Roosevelt reached an agreement on this issue.

I had the satisfaction of seeing many of our recommendations included in the final executive agreement, but the media later commented on many cases of mistreatment or exploitation of the Mexican workers. Nevertheless, the Mexicans I talked to years later, including my chauffeur and an office worker, had nothing but good things to say about their experience. The long lines of workers trying to be accepted at the Mexican processing centers seemed to prove that there was excess labor and that their previous experiences across the border weren't too unsatisfactory.

Typically, however, we didn't spend very much time initiating legislation, or debating the merits of executive proposals in the chamber. In fact, during my entire three-year term, of the more than one hundred executive bills introduced, not a single one was defeated, although one communications bill was filed, not to be taken up until late in the successive legislative session in 1946. In contrast, if a deputy introduces a bill, which happens relatively infrequently, they pass only about one-third of the time. Our debates over presidential programs, similar to our debates over candidates for office, took place privately, in this case, in the committees. This is why most Mexicans believe nothing goes on in the chamber. We do work, it's just hidden from view. I believe that's why attendance at the general sessions isn't taken seriously. On many days, we couldn't obtain a quorum. We didn't have the staff or expertise to compete with the executive branch on legislation, a situation that has weakened the chamber in relation to executive authority. Some of my colleagues in recent years have suggested we repeal the no reelection provision as applied to congress. They believe that long seniority in the chamber will enhance congressional expertise. In my three years in the chamber, we amended one bill in committee. I made some suggestions in the Labor Committee, and since other members agreed with my arguments, our chairman broached the proposed changes with the president of the Gran Comisión. He called together the experts of the Secretariats of Labor and Industry and Commerce, and we debated various interpretations. When the Gran Comisión approved half of our proposed changes, we considered ourselves victorious. Similarly, the chamber as a whole passed the bill without debate. Other than this bill, the chamber was neither instrumental in deciding the amount of funding allocated to specific projects, nor in determining the gist of legislation.

I spent most of my time seeing people and groups from my home district. In particular, we assisted less fortunate Mexicans in our constituencies. As the state delegation leader, I had even greater numbers of persons waiting to see me, some from areas outside of my old district. The majority of their requests involved promised public works, land disputes, and job opportunities for needy individuals. One of my more memorable experiences as a deputy occurred during my second year in office. Hernán Romero, my father's close friend and *compadre*, came to Mexico City representing Purépero. After paying his respects to my mother, he arrived at my office early one morning, before I had come in. As I entered the back door, my secretary gave me a slip of paper with his name on it, saying with a smile that "he says you're an old friend." Her smile was prompted by the fact that many who sought an audience with me to ask for something implied they knew me. In this situation, of course, it was true. I told her to bring him right in.

He moved slowly through the entrance way, his back slightly bent. I embraced him. In my grasp his frame felt brittle and light, but his return embrace was firm.

"Look at you!" he exclaimed, sweeping the room with a motion of his hand, "how far you have come since I sent you off to Morelia so many years ago. God has rewarded my faith in you." He dabbed the outside corners of his eyes with a rumpled handkerchief, removing the tiny trickle of tears common to

172

many men his age. "Your mama is so proud of you. You have been a good son to her. If only your papa were alive to see you, to share in her pride."

"Yes, I know, I think of that, too," I said. "And your family, *compadre*, how are they?"

"As well as could be expected, *joven*," he nodded, removing a piece of lint from the lapel of his traditional, black wool suit. His white shirt, with yellowed buttons, had gone through many washings, but it was clean.

Our talk continued with many personal reminiscences, as Romero gradually worked his way to the purpose of his visit.

"Education was so important to your success, *joven*."

"Yes, not just important, but crucial, don't you think?" I asked.

"This is true, which is why I'm here, my old friend."

"Oh, really, please explain," I motioned, opening my palms outward.

"Well," said the old man, clearing his throat, "we need a much larger school in Purépero. The town is growing. School-children are plentiful, but the space is too small. Many of your friends now have children in school, and they and others asked me to come here and request your help. Can the government give us a larger school?"

"Ah, my friend, that's a worthwhile need, and your question is a fair one, but difficult to answer," I explained. "There are so many Mexicans without schools, teachers, books. I know you don't exaggerate, that you represent a real need in my *pueblo*. The problem is how to meet the needs of all of our people."

"Of course you're right, but maybe we could still be among the first to benefit from the government's school program. A wonderful way for you to repay your people, and repeat your own opportunity, would be to obtain a school for Purépero," he ended, with emotion pervading his words.

Placing both hands on the edge of my desk, I replied, "I can

173

make no promises to you, Hernán. But for you and my people, I will talk to friends in the ministry and see what they will do. Is that satisfactory?"

"Very much so," said Hernán gladly. "I have faith in you. I'm sure you will succeed. Purépero will forever be in your debt."

"Thank you for your confidence, *compadre*, but be patient, these things take time," I cautioned him.

Despite this warning, he left with an air of optimism. Several weeks later, after breakfast with a group of former Vasconcelistas, I cornered an old friend of José Vasconcelos who had become Avila Camacho's Minister of Public Education in 1941. When I asked if we could talk he offered to give me a ride in his chauffered automobile. It was here that I broached the subject my *compadre* had addressed earlier.

"Mr. Secretary, a delegation from my *pueblo*," I exaggerated, "approached me several weeks ago about a new school program. I know school building funds are needed throughout Mexico, and I do believe this is equally true in my *pueblo*. If this is so, would it be possible for you to have the department in charge allocate building funds there as a priority location?"

"Anything is possible, Toño. It's a reasonable request. If your hometown does have an equal need, there's no reason why we cannot move it to the top of our list. I can look into it for you," he added agreeably.

"That's all I ask, Mr. Secretary, just a consideration of it as a possibility."

"Of course, Toño, I can make no guarantee, even though it's a small matter."

"Yes, yes, I understand," giving my assent. "One never knows, even with the simplest requests."

Several weeks later the Minister's private secretary called to say that Purépero was eligible for funds under the building program and that it would be put at the top of the list for schools in Michoacán. The department head in charge of the program would notify me in several weeks when official approval had been granted. My personal intervention had succeeded in moving the bureaucratic wheels forward, the means by which all decisions are accomplished in Mexico. I had actually forgotten about the notification, when, several months later, I received a polite letter from Romero asking me if I had been able to make any inquiries. I called the department head to ask about the status of the project in light of the previous instructions I had received. He was not in, and I was forced to discuss the matter with his secretary.

"I wish to know if the funds have been officially approved for the school construction project in Purépero? The minister's office informed me several months ago that I would receive some notification from your department. Could you leave a message with your boss?" I requested.

"Of course, I'm sure he will be able to give you a response once he's out of a meeting. Rest assured, we'll return your call."

I thanked the secretary and hung up the phone. It was several days before I heard from the office again. I was out, and my secretary indicated to me that the program was still being "considered," and that there had been some "delays." Impatient with this vacillating, I phoned once again.

"One moment please, *Licenciado*, let me see if he's in." A pause, and then the woman's voice came on the line again. "He's in a meeting, sir, please allow me to call his secretary."

Annoyed I brusquely replied, "Please do!"

Two clicks, and the obsequious voice of the secretary came on the line. "Ah, Mr. Deputy, I'm sorry my boss is gone again. What can I do for you?"

"I received your message concerning my earlier questions about the school-construction project in Purépero. I'm puzzled by the delay, what's the problem?"

"Well, sir," he paused, "I'm not sure exactly, but these things

175

take time. There are many other projects that need simultaneous consideration. Perhaps all the necessary information isn't available for a final decision."

"What information are you referring to?" I asked. "This is the first time I have heard about that."

"Oh, well, ah, I mean," he stumbled, "I meant information about the student population, the availability of other structures, the number of teachers, all of those facts necessary for consideration."

"But," I queried, "doesn't this city qualify for the program?"

"Yes, yes," he replied, "but these things must be considered too."

Undaunted, I suggested that those data were what had already determined Purépero's status for official consideration.

The secretary paused, clearing his throat repeatedly, "Well, I'm not exactly sure. You see. . ."

I interrupted, "I want to speak to your boss about this. I want clarification."

"As you wish, Sir, I was only trying to help."

"Please have him call me at his earliest convenience," I replied abruptly, hanging up the phone.

No word came from his office. After waiting two more weeks, then trying to speak with him, and again being put off by the department head, I called the minister. He brought up the subject of my original request himself, without prompting from me; he wondered if I was satisfied with the work his office had done. Politely, I explained that while I had been very pleased with his help, the matter seemed to have come to a dead end in the department in charge of the building program. He genuinely seemed surprised and promised to have the matter investigated immediately.

The next day my secretary buzzed to say that the minister was on the phone. I picked up the receiver and greeted him.

"I have news about your project my friend. It seems as though one of your colleagues in the Chamber, who is a *compadre* of my *oficial mayor*, made a similar request for a town in his district. The *oficial mayor* asked that his request be given preference, and seeing that you were both *diputados*, and not being well informed of my interest in the matter, my department head naturally favored the other project, and tried to avoid dealing with your request."

"I see," I replied, knowingly.

"But don't concern yourself, the situation is clearly understood now, your project is officially approved, and you will receive a letter from that office next week indicating that to you. So, you may inform your constituents."

"Thank you for your time and interest in this. I'm sorry to have caused you all this trouble," I told him.

"Don't worry, Toño, for a friend it's nothing."

Shortly afterward my friend was replaced as the Minister of Education. But the new minister, committed to an expanded educational program, permitted the project to be completed; to my surprise and personal satisfaction, Purépero would have its new school.

24

Nomination
Time

As the end of my term in the legislature grew nearer, I began planning to return full-time to my law practice, which blossomed during my partial absence. We added several more lawyers, students I groomed from my labor-law course. Amado had carefully nurtured the office along during my campaign and legislative duties. In 1943, political rumors circulated in the newspapers concerning the upcoming candidates for the governorship of Michoacán. I saw my name in print as a possible candidate, and I laughed, knowing that I wasn't a serious contender. But many believed the rumors, for who could know in our highly secretive system who the real candidate was.

Several months later, in the midst of these press rumors, I received a phone call from Germán Torres saying that as state party chairman, he and other leaders wanted to promote me for governor. Would I accept their offer for support? My reaction was hesitant. Of course, to become the highest official of your home state is a dream any politically active Mexican would like to fulfill. It was a secret ambition in the back of my mind. Also, one always is flattered to have political friends think you deserve such a post. I said that my chances were not very good, that I was indeed a dark horse candidate, but that if he wanted to stir up the political waters a bit to see what filtered out, I would permit him to promote my candidacy. After all, Germán was a professional politician who knew the climate of our home state. If he thought the present governor's favorite lacked strong support, perhaps my chances were better than I had believed.

Political reporters frequently mentioned eight names as possible candidates. My competition included a lawyer who was then Secretary-General of Government in Michoacán, and thought to be the Governor's first choice for the nomination; a former textile mechanic who had not exercised his profession since becoming the local leader of the CTM nearly twelve years ago; a physician, director of the state medical services; a lawyer and former senator, in the race for a third time; another lawyer and member of the Supreme Court; a civil engineer serving as *Oficial Mayor* of the public works ministry; and a military officer serving as zone commander of Michoacán. As the weeks went by, our ranks in the state political news shifted up and down depending on what piece of information most recently surfaced.

Two of my media friends joined Germán to promote my campaign for the nomination. In Michoacán, Leopoldo organized a group called *Profesionistas Pro-Gutiérrez* for governor, using his contacts among doctors and other professional people. They took out ads in the regional papers. In Mexico City, Andrés moved on two fronts, creating the *Abogados Michoacanos, A.C.*, association to organize former Michoacanos who were residing in Mexico City to support my candidacy. Also, several of the younger lawyers from our firm found sympathetic students in the residential house for National University students in Mexico City. Advertisements appeared in the major dailies and our Michoacán newsletter.

About a month before the nomination was to be announced, a number of candidates dropped from the race. Remaining in the running were the Secretary-General, belonging to the clique of the present governor; the *Oficial Mayor*, considered to have the indirect support of the President because of his friendship with the President's brother; and lastly, my name was moved up from dark horse status to one of three, a *terna*. The press confused the source of my strength since they thought I was tied to Cárdenas's mafia, even though the governor himself was part of that group.

The political situation in Michoacán was unsettled. The incumbent governor, a revolutionary general, had been attacked repeatedly for abusing his position. This is in part why the one military candidate had no chance for the nomination. Further, although in these decisions the President wielded ultimate authority, Michoacán was considered by all to be Cárdenas's territory. During World War II President Avila Camacho invited Cárdenas back into the government to take charge of the defense ministry. I didn't know how the President would perceive me, especially in relation to the others. I saw my chances as slim, following the same rationale which appeared in one of many news stories in *El Universal:*

The final *terna* seems well entrenched just weeks before the candidate will be announced in Morelia; these candidates include: Lic. Antonio Gutiérrez, of the firm Gutiérrez and Cosío, recently a deputy from Purépero; Ing. Fernando Morales, *Oficial Mayor* of Public Works, closely tied to the President's brother, Maximino; and Lic. Pedro Flores Ramírez, *compadre* of the present governor. Recent comments by expert observers suggest that Morales is the favorite. It has been suggested that Morales will obtain the nomination because Gutiérrez and Flores Ramírez are competing for the same source of support. A likely compromise candidate, who through his contacts can bring more economic projects to Michoacán, is Flores Ramírez. Locally, the candidacy of. . . .

Part Five

The commentator seemed to have struck a truth there. Since we both had support from the Cárdenas group, the choice of either one of us would offend at least some members of the Cárdenas *camarilla*. I hadn't talked to the General to see where he stood on the issue.

On a Monday morning soon after this article appeared, I received a call from the Ministry of Government. The minister wanted to see me. I made an appointment for the following afternoon. My companion from the preparatory school, Miguel Alemán, still held that post. His secretary did not say what Alemán wanted to discuss with me.

The next day my driver took me to the ministry, a long, low colonial building fronted by a high, iron fence. At the gate, the guard stopped us momentarily while the driver gave my name. We whisked through to the inner courtyard. Even though this position was second only to that of President in political importance, the office was not all that impressive. I gave my name to the porter who scurried off to inform the minister's secretary of my arrival. When he returned, he invited me into his office for coffee. We chatted briefly about the state of politics and events in Europe. The buzzer on his phone sounded unobtrusively, and he interrupted our conversation to announce that Alemán was ready to see me. Alemán, immaculately and tastefully dressed, as was his custom, greeted me warmly with the usual pleasantries and inquiries about my family's well-being. Leading up gracefully to the point of our meeting, he changed the direction of our conversation, clearing his throat.

"I've asked you here today to personally give you some good news."

"Yes, Miguel," I said, straightening in my chair, "what is it?"

"The President wishes you to know that you will be the next Governor of Michoacán."

I gulped, inaudibly, asking almost rhetorically aloud, "Is it true?"

He chuckled softly. "You're surprised, no?"

"Truthfully, yes. It must show."

"A little, Toño," he said understandingly, "just a little bit."

Regaining my composure somewhat, and remembering my political manners, I asked him to convey to the President "my most grateful appreciation for his confidence in me, and my promise to live up to that trust with responsibility."

"I will be pleased to pass on your message, and I'm sure he'll receive it well," replied Alemán.

I thanked him, feeling more relaxed.

"One thought, Toño," cautioned my friend, "you must remember that the official announcement has not yet been made. That will not happen for a week or so, and therefore, you should keep this news to yourself."

"Yes, of course, I will tell no one."

"Good. If I can be of service during your campaign, please call on me."

A few minutes later, after conversing further with his private secretary, I left the building. It seems odd to me that at moments like that, when you are overwhelmed with good news, that you still wonder why. Many years later in a conversation with the President's private secretary, I received a logical explanation to my polite inquiry as to why Morales did not receive the President's nod of approval.

My friend laughed, "That was a difficult choice for the President. You see, Maximino was pressuring him to give it to Morales. But Cárdenas had no use for Morales, for what reason I'm not sure. Anyway, the President wasn't about to alienate Cárdenas, even if his brother was Morales's patron."

"Well, that explains why Morales didn't get it. But why not Flores Ramírez, the governor's candidate?"

"Ah," he said, knowingly, rubbing his hands together,

"that's where the President made his craftiest move."

"How?"

"Well, you both had ties to General Cárdenas, no?"

"Yes, but Flores Ramírez's were much closer than mine."

"Correct, but that's exactly his weakness and your strength."

"In what sense, *hombre*?"

"In order not to offend his brother, Avila Camacho could rationalize Cárdenas's strong objections to Morales. Being a realist, Maximino, although upset with not having his choice accepted, understood the reasoning behind his brother's rejection. But, to make the decision more palatable, the President chooses you, because while you're not Cárdenas's first choice, you're respected by him and completely acceptable. Thus, Cárdenas cannot complain to the President, and yet the President can tell his brother that Cárdenas isn't getting his first choice either. And most important, the President is able to show his independence decisively, deflecting criticism that he is unduly influenced by either Cárdenas or his brother."

"So that's it," I sighed.

"Yes, do you see the logic in it?"

"Of course," I replied, "very clearly."

"I hope I haven't offended you in telling the story, I mean, about your position in all this."

"No, no, *hombre*. Frankly, I could never quite understand it myself. I always had thought my chances were behind the others."

"Yes, but they played by the rules, too. They were rewarded for their patience. Morales later got the subsecretary post in the ministry. Flores Ramírez became a senator. So, you see, it all worked out well in the end."

It did. What strange enigmas are cast by our political logic.

25

La
Patria Chica

The election was a foregone conclusion. I had no opposition. On September 16, 1944, I became the new governor of Michoacán. It was a gala affair. The President sent Cárdenas to represent him at my inauguration. Also present among the crowd of well-wishers were numerous former governors of the state, including Francisco Múgica. The national legislature was well represented by several deputies and one of our senators. I gave a long speech to this audience of notables, setting forth my social and economic goals, and promising to listen to the requests of all the state's citizens.

Prior to my election, Michoacán, and all other Mexican states, had changed their gubernatorial tenure from a four-year term to a six-year term. I was the first governor to benefit from this extension, and since under the state constitution I could not be reelected to the governorship, this was an important revision which gave me extra time to achieve my many plans. Several days after my election, I revealed to the press the names of my collaborators. To act as my most important subordinate, Secretary-General of Government, I designated Germán. Although he was reluctant to become more directly involved in the administrative and political aspects of public health, I persuaded Leopoldo Vela to become Director of Health Services. For two other important positions, I sought out old friends who had remained in Michoacán these many years. Ramón Martínez, my first friend in Morelia, had achieved his goal of receiving a degree in engineering in his mid-thirties. He had been working as a supervisor of the National Highway Commission in the western part of Michoacán. He was pleased to become my Director of Public Works. Silvestre Vázquez, "El Indio," my old companion from San Nicolás, had completed his law degree at the University of Guadalajara and had entered private practice in Morelia. He twice had been a city councilman, and ran successfully for the state legislature. It was an easy choice to ask him to serve as head of the legislature. For Director of the State Police force, I chose an army official recommended to me by my predecessor, himself a career officer.

Winning the governorship required some changes in our social and personal life. Emma had given birth to a second child, a son Antonio, and was pregnant with our third. We kept our house in San Angel, leaving it in charge of a housekeeper and gardener. I travelled constantly between the capital and Morelia on state business, and Emma often accompanied me to visit her family. Our contacts with friends in Mexico City were less frequent, but they were still regular. And, since Morelia's beauty as a tranquil colonial city was popular among urbanites, an occasional friend would come to stay with us.

I had great plans for my state. There was much to do, and many agencies were available to me to accomplish my dreams. I hoped to raise the pace of development through increased educational facilities, better health care, and improved transportation. The latter was crucial since we had few well developed industries, and commercial activity could only increase through improved transportation north and east, tying us with the capital and the highway between Mexico and Guadalajara. A sizable portion of our revenues were monies the federal government returned to us from taxes. For additional funds, Michoacán, like all states, had to seek out federal projects in public works, communications, social services, and other areas.

Before taking office I had not realized how limited the state's resources were. I understood that handling the political pressures in my own state would largely depend on my ability to compete with other governors for coveted funds. Many governors applied their political skills to smooth over their local problems, but I realized that my forte was obtaining new resources and using them administratively to resolve our problems. Therefore, I let Germán oversee the day-to-day political manuevering, while I concentrated my efforts on acquiring new resources. The first year in office I had a difficult time since I knew only two ministers on a personal basis: Lázaro Cárdenas in Defense and Jaime Torres Bodet, who had been Vasconcelos's disciple, in Education.

Most important among the federal officials who controlled funds was the Treasury minister, Eduardo Suárez, a Cardenista and a holdover from his administration. I did not know him personally, but he had a reputation for efficiency and integrity. Public works became one of my primary vehicles for development, but I had to use state funds since the President's brother was still minister of Public Works, and he hardly looked upon my requests with a favorable eye. Along with the necessity of competing for federal funds with other states came the local pressure from the municipalities, whose funds were scarcer and came primarily from state coffers. As one of my colleagues crudely expressed this relationship, "The federal government screws me, and I screw the city governments."

Early in my term, while on a trip to Mexico City, I succeeded in persuading Torres Bodet to visit Michoacán to see our efforts to build more schools. He fulfilled his promise and, on his next tour, spent several days in Michoacán. Knowing it was necessary to impress him with the seriousness of our efforts, I carefully prepared for his visit.

Torres Bodet was not typical of the ministers in Avila Camacho's cabinet. He was only five years older than I, and he had risen quickly throughout his career. He had spent many of his younger days abroad in the foreign service, after serving as Vasconcelos's private secretary at the age of nineteen, while I was still in preparatory school. Initially he had been Subsecretary of Foreign Relations in the cabinet; but midway, in 1943, at the age of forty-one, the President appointed him Secretary of Public Education. Truly an intellectual, he published many poems in the 1920s, which gave him national prominence. During his visit I approached him about one of my plans as we sat in my patio, enjoying the bright sun and refreshing breeze of a typical Morelian summer afternoon.

We sipped *café de olla,* a spicy, sugary drink. "Tell me, Antonio," he asked, "do you have any special plans to promote our national literacy program?"

I told him I did, that I wanted to give a different emphasis to state educational programs by concentrating on educating teachers, rather than on constructing primary schools or substantially increasing university funding.

"What did you have in mind?" he asked.

Encouraged by his interest I continued. "Well, I hope to promote the normal program, to build on its basic strength but expand the facility to make normal education our principal focus."

"The need for teachers is definite. But," and he paused, forming the words slowly with large lips unusual for a Mexican, "there will be pressures to build more schools. How will you cope with these, my friend?"

I had anticipated this question and had an answer ready. "I

188

have discussed this matter with some of my advisors. Building more schools has, of course, been the usual approach. But I think we have to ask for a commitment from the *pueblo*. After all, nothing is sacrificed if we provide the school, even if they sometimes do the construction themselves. So, my idea is this. The village needs to provide a building for the schoolroom and for the teacher's living quarters. We, on the other hand, will provide them with the teacher, and with some of the materials. They cannot supply the teacher, but they are more able to supply the materials and the labor for the facilities."

"That's an interesting approach," he mused.

"Perhaps we could experiment with it in a certain region," I urged.

"Yes, that might be wise. I would like to consider it further. I will respond to your suggestion when I return to Mexico City."

"Fine, fine, it's just something I wanted to suggest," I replied, agreeing to his request for more time.

It was difficult to know how our funds compared with other states, but the next year's allotment from the Secretariat of Public Education was much better than in previous years. As promised, I did receive a further communication from the secretary saying that he thought my proposal had merit, and that he would bolster our monies to facilitate experimentation. Some of my political advisers were not keen on this project because it depended heavily on persuading villagers to come forth with extra effort. They argued that the people had come to rely heavily on the government for results, rather than on self-help, and that this program would fail if the government's representatives couldn't convince them of its benefits and of the state's commitment. The program was successful, but truthfully, only moderately, for some of the reasons my advisers suggested. At the time, however, it never occurred to them or to me that the political effects of this program would be nearly disastrous to my administration.

189

Two years into my term, the rectorship of the Colegio de San Nicolás came up for reelection. As usual, student groups vociferously supported various representatives. One of those candidates was Leopoldo, who since the completion of his degree had taught courses in medicine. I strongly encouraged him in his efforts, and when he was selected as one of the *terna* for the office, I gladly chose him as rector.

As rector, Leopoldo supported my general education program by giving an increased emphasis to the normal teaching program. We always seemed to be short of funds for worthy projects, but within the university, the normal school received generous support. This condition became obvious to regular university students who began to raise complaints to the university council, saying that other programs should receive increased funding. Our initial attempts to allay their fears were successful. But toward the last year of my administration, Leopoldo was up again for reelection. He was popular with his own faculty and with the normal students, but a group centered in the law school and in the preparatory program supported another candidate. I publicly came out in support of Leopoldo.

The student politics behind the election began to heat up. And, as in my own student days, the importance of the issues to the students grew disproportionately to their real impact. In order to tie the rector's failures and the educational program's weaknesses more directly to me, students dredged up the accusation that Cementos Michoacanos, S.A., had received many of the contracts for construction supplies made available to the villages. They implied this had something to do with the fact that my firm represented Cementos Michoacanos in Mexico City. It was true that I worked for them for many years, and that my firm was still their representative, but I never awarded those contracts personally. It was just a scurrilous campaign on the part of the students to put us, and more directly Leopoldo, on the defensive.

One evening in the midst of these vicious attacks the police chief asked to see me.

"Governor, the students have asked permission to march to the *zócalo* near the cathedral. How should I respond to their request?"

"Chief," I instructed, "if you expect them to be orderly and nonviolent, give them official permission. I think you should put out extra forces just in case, but don't provoke them."

"Yes, Governor, we can do that. But I think it's outrageous how they've treated you these past months, especially their leader, who's a punk, a real rabble-rouser. I'd like to take care of him for you once and for all. He's scum," he said with an angry scowl, "and would better understand this," he said, affectionately patting the butt of his pistol.

"Your concern is appreciated. I understand how you feel, but that's not the way to deal with people. He has a right to disagree with our policies," I lectured. "Don't worry, we can beat him with our organization, our supporters, and the press."

"I hope you're right, Governor. The son of a bitch doesn't deserve your respectful treatment."

"Perhaps, Chief, but I prefer it this way."

As the competition for the rectorship came closer to the deadline for a recommendation from the university council, vociferous student unrest became more worrisome. I wanted to see my loyal collaborators have a good chance at the federal elective posts for which the official nominations were to be announced shortly. Germán was a candidate for federal deputy from his home district, and I was pushing several other friends for deputyships, too. But the President of Mexico, now Alemán, even though my friend, would not be disposed to favor my candidates if I could not bring about a resolution to these problems. Bad publicity never helps a politician's career in the eyes of his superior. I wasn't afraid of slander, and I believed the easiest way to cope with this problem was to ride out the election of the rectorship and let the issue die with it. But that wasn't to happen.

Just a week before the election the student leader referred to by the police chief disappeared. The press, sniffing a good story, ran banner headlines the next day. His student friends claimed he was forced into a car by two men, one of whom they alleged was a policeman. Immediately I was deluged with accusations as the instigator of the crime. I waited a day to see if he would turn up. Then I held a press conference, and announced that I personally had asked the state attorney general to investigate the matter. A month later, with the help of a federal agent, two policemen were charged with kidnapping the boy. According to their story, they had forced him into the car, intending only to scare him. But when they had let him out, he spoke defiantly against their actions, and one of the policemen struck his forehead so forcefully with a billy club that the impact of the blow knocked the student down, bashing in the back of his head as it struck the car's front fender. Scared, they dumped his body off a trail leading from one of the many logging roads in the mountains. It was found by a peasant several weeks later.

Under interrogation by the attorney general, one of the policemen broke down, saying he had been under orders from the police chief to terrorize the student. My attorney general came to me with the confession. I knew it looked bad, but I insisted that we announce that charges had been made against the two policemen and their chief, too. I called him in and dismissed him. He was remorseful, saying only that he had wanted neither me nor my collaborators to suffer outrageous accusations. But his loyalty was misguided, and I had no idea he would do

something like that. I think he believed I would protect him for removing a thorn from my side. But in place of an irritation, he created a wave of revulsion among the populace, something I would have to overcome. I believe my quick application of the law to the offenders, and their subsequent conviction, did much to allay the suspicions of most people. But my enemies never would believe I had nothing to do with the crime. To this day I'm still haunted by the memory of that unfortunate boy.

26

The Cabinet

In September 1950, six years to the day after my inauguration, I relinquished my position as governor of Michoacán. At
first I felt relieved of a heavy responsibility. Then I was bored.
We moved back to Mexico City to our residence in San Angel.
I returned full-time to my legal practice. I began to spend some
of my seemingly endless leisure time on intellectual activities.
In 1952, one of my former law professors, Luis Garrido Díaz,
who had been elected Rector of the National University, asked
me to return to my *alma mater* to teach a course on labor law.
This I did gladly, for I liked the challenge of teaching and the
discussions with the students.

For the first year following my return to the practice of law I
stayed away from political activity. But as the guessing game
for the presidential candidate began in earnest in 1951, I instinctively began a search for a likely contender for the nomination, someone I should support. I knew most of Alemán's
cabinet since half a dozen had been my teachers at the National Law School in the 1930s. Two of my former professors
were early leading contenders: Fernando Casas Alemán, the

head of the Department of the Federal District, and Ramón Beteta, Secretary of the Treasury.

Early rumors in the newspapers named Casas Alemán the strongest contender, and he himself acted as if he already had the nod from the President. But, although many of the president's collaborators were already throwing their support to Casas Alemán, I personally felt more comfortable with Beteta, a man whose social conscience was closer to my own. He had been an early adviser to Cárdenas, and was one of the few politicians to make the transition from Cárdenas to Alemán. Events moved quickly and Casas Alemán's support disappeared, as if a slap in the face for his overconfidence. I, too, misjudged, since Beteta was unsatisfactory. Of course no one will ever really know why except perhaps Miguel Alemán, but political pundits claimed Beteta was too close to the Alemán group and that he was too pro-American, including being married to a North American. Alemán's Secretary of Interior, Ruiz Cortines, "the old man," received the designation. Ruiz Cortines came from a different generation than the rest of the president's supporters. His candidacy left me frozen, outside the political arena. I had no connections with his group. No one would be looking out for my political ambitions over the next six years except me.

I dedicated myself to my other affairs with renewed enthusiasm. I became increasingly active in my long-neglected professional organizations. The Seminar of Mexican Culture asked me to become a numbered member, confirming, I thought, the prestige of my recent activities. I renewed the regular breakfast meetings with old friends as well as with several more recent acquaintances. The conversations were lively and we exchanged all sorts of recent political gossip. Since Andrés had been elected a senator from Michoacán in 1952, his political contributions were the most informed.

Several years after the start of the Ruiz Cortines administration I received a note from Adolfo López Mateos, the Secretary of Labor, asking me for advice on several pending changes in the federal labor law. I had known him as a student when we both campaigned for Vasconcelos in his abortive attempt for the presidency. We conversed several times about the legal changes themselves, and the Secretary asked me for written suggestions. Using the research assistance of several of my best students, one of whom was interning at our law offices, I compiled a report. López Mateos was pleased with my recommendations, and asked if I would be willing to serve as his advisor. I gladly acceded to his request, and received a monthly salary that was most generous for the services I provided.

Intermixed with my consulting activities and regular law practice, I completed a textbook on labor law which Porrúa, the elite private house, decided to publish. In two years it sold out the first edition and went into a second printing. My academic efforts were rewarded with an invitation from the Dean to teach a seminar on labor law for the recently instituted doctorate of laws program. In 1956, having taught at the National Law School for a number of years prior to my election as governor, I was sufficiently recognized to be appointed to the Governing Board of the National University, joining several of my former professors, colleagues, and student companions. This brought me back more directly into the politics of the University, and into the process of selecting a rector, which fortunately only came up once in the next decade.

The years which followed added little to my political experiences. I enjoyed the intellectual pursuits, but itched to get back into political life. But six years is a very short time. Soon *the event* in Mexican politics, that of presidential succession, was on everyone's lips. As in the past I knew several of the precandidates personally, although my only political tie during the early maneuvering was with López Mateos. This was a fortuitous circumstance since he became one of the front-runners.

I decided to remain loyal to him, hoping he had the inside track. To demonstrate my interest in his presidential ambitions, I organized a group of lawyers, primarily in labor law, to support his precandidacy and to entertain him for dinner. He graciously accepted, and the affair went off rather well.

To my personal pleasure López Mateos, as history has recorded, became the official party candidate for President in late 1957. As part of his campaign retinue he asked me if I would direct a committee to deal with contemporary labor problems and listen to the complaints of the working class. I accepted his offer, and travelled to numerous cities with him, holding sessions with labor-union representatives. The opposition candidate, Luis Héctor Alvarez, a stalwart Panista and prominent businessman from Chihuahua, frequently attacked the labor movement, particularly the official unions. His one-sided criticisms made labor corruption a frequent campaign issue. I invited several of my colleagues from the University to participate in traveling seminars, and at the end of the campaign, I wrote up a series of reports for López Mateos, who roundly defeated Alvarez for the presidency.

I expected to receive some reward for my support of López Mateos, perhaps in the form of a high position in the labor secretariat. But only the president-elect himself knew who his choices would be. Rumors began to fly among his closest collaborators, but they were just that, rumors. Jaime Torres Bodet, who had remained a good friend from my days as governor, called to inform me in mid-November that the president-elect had asked him to be Secretary of Public Education, for the second time. He said he thought I would receive the Secretariat of Labor. Two days later I received a phone call from López Mateos's secretary asking me to come to his home in the morning.

I arrived a little early. Waiting in a luxurious parlour, I examined the fine, French furniture and the ornate, decorative crafts. My wait was brief. The new President was a handsome man, his dark, wavy hair glistening with brillantine, combed back from a slightly receding hairline along his temples. Gregarious by nature, his demeanor seemed warm and inviting. He greeted me enthusiastically.

"Sit down, sit down, *hombre.* I appreciate your final reports. They'll be most useful to my administration. Many of your observations coincide with my own," said the President, smiling.

"I'm glad they could be of some use," I replied.

"They have, my friend," and he paused, becoming more serious, "but I'm hoping you will continue to contribute to your country by assisting in other ways."

"I'd be pleased to serve in any capacity, Mr. President."

"Good, that's what I expected to hear from you," he said, settling back in his chair. "I have an important task for you, Toño, I'd like you to take over the Social Security Institute. Will you do it?"

"Of course, it would be an honor to serve in your administration in such a capacity."

He smiled broadly at my response, nodding his head and rubbing his chin with his left hand. "It'll be a challenge for you. I hope to expand coverage to more workers and increase the types of services our system can provide. The economy is growing rapidly, but we can't rest on our past achievements."

"I agree," I replied. "Our fellow citizens often forget that this concept was one of the most unique and far-reaching labor reforms in the 1917 Constitution. We need to continue progressive efforts to compensate for the delay in initiating social services until 1944. I'd be proud to have a part in their expansion."

"Excellent, then I can count on you?"

I assured him he could.

199

Part Five

"Any questions, Toño?"

"May I have the liberty to choose my immediate subordinates?" I asked.

"In your agency, yes. I'm not predisposed to recommend anyone as your Secretary-General. Most of your other directors require some technical expertise. Your predecessor will be an important member of my cabinet, and I recommend that you seek some advice from him," he cautioned. "Please call him about the details of moving in."

And with that thought our interview came to an end. So, I was to become a member of the President's team. My days on the outside looking in were over. Once again I would have to think about gathering together a group of collaborators. My decisions did not require long deliberation. Andrés Bustamante had left the Senate. I asked him to join me as my immediate subordinate. For Director of Medical Services I called on Leopoldo Vela, who, for the first time, left his native Michoacán to come to Mexico City. He jumped at the opportunity to design some health-care programs for social-security recipients. I put several of my brightest young law students into other administrative positions.

We moved into spacious offices overlooking the Paseo de la Reforma just above the sensuous statue of Diana, the huntress, which then marked the boundary of Chapultepec Park. That same day the President called us together in an unusual cabinet meeting. It was a private session; even his military aide waited outside the door. He admonished us with a general warning and fatherly advice.

"Friends," he said, "you now hold the most important positions in your country's government. You have a special responsibility to me and to the people. Your job is to fulfill the duties and responsibilities of your office, to see that the policies of the government are implemented. I don't care how many mistresses you have, or what time you come to your

200

office, that is your business, but I want those obligations carried out, however best you can achieve them."

Some of the President's collaborators complied with his request to the best of their abilities; many did not, either because they lacked the skill or the commitment. I honestly felt my agency achieved most of our goals during his term. The success of my program not only depended on the efficiency of my personal staff, but on the receipt of funds from the treasury for the expansion of current programs. Instead of competing with other states, as I had done as governor, I now found myself competing with other cabinet members for the President's ear and the funds dispensed by the Treasury Secretary. The political intrigues entailed in this competition were complex, but fortunately the President did not encourage divisiveness, a style that regrettably did characterize Luis Echeverría's administration. I assumed the President, if he favored my projects, would always make the funds available. I quickly learned, however, that he used the Treasury Secretary as a neutral evaluator. Only if the President had a strong personal interest in something would he tell the Secretary to make the funds available. My long acquaintance with the Secretary going back to our preparatory school days working on *Eureka* helped my efforts to persuade him. But there were times when he would just tell me that "no funds were available." Generally, though, my initiatives were funded and the official reports of my administration document statistically my achievements as Director General.

The most important policy issue of my administration was the question of broadening social-security coverage. The population during the 1960s and 1970s was increasing faster than we could afford to expand coverage. Naturally, the pressure of this growth had an impact on all other programs. Only the President could set priorities, but it was very difficult to get the President's ear because he didn't hold joint cabinet sessions. Occasionally several of us were called in to discuss a related policy issue. Several intracabinet coordinating committees existed to encourage cooperation. Typically, however, we operated independently of one another, each agency competing for presidential attention.

In the middle of his administration, I tried to focus the president's attention on expanding social-security coverage, including both the retirement and medical-care program, in rural areas. I realized that our programs in the cities were incomplete, but the condition of the peasant, relatively speaking, was worse than his urban counterpart. As part of my overall philosophy, it seemed that we needed to send a message to the rural population that the government, and indeed society, cared about them. After all our efforts in land reform, my arguments in law school with my friends still applied—we were providing insufficient credit, investment, and technical expertise to the small farmer. I had no control over those policies, but I hoped to stimulate renewed vigor in the agrarian sector through an activist social policy. My colleagues in the Agrarian Department and the Agricultural Ministry supported my arguments to the President.

My staff provided careful studies to illustrate the long-term benefits of even a small program. López Mateos was not unsympathetic. Like Cárdenas, he accelerated the land-distribution program. Ultimately, and I'm willing to admit it in these pages, I failed. I'm not blind to the reasons. One view toward rural interests has prevailed, and still does, within our ruling elite. That view, which has nearly always maintained its hegemony in governmental policy, is to implement programs favorable to urban interests. The logic behind this attitude was sensible. The rate of urbanization was extraordinary during these years. Urban residents were more sophisticated about their political demands. Recognizing these demands, our leaders allocated disproportionate resources to urban states and to the cities in general, hoping to ameliorate discontent. I've always felt, too, that the lack of sympathy for rural problems, when it comes to giving out public resources, has to do with the fact that few of my colleagues, unlike myself, come from rural, peasant backgrounds. I'm sure that one's origins influence decisions on the distribution of resources.

This urban bias has been most unfortunate. Every administration points to its rural reforms as achievements. I don't deny they have been quite real. But overall, the gap has grown between the traditional agricultural and industrial sectors. It's not just a question of monetary or physical resources, but also a question of emotional support. We have failed to recognize the psychological value of providing our peasants with recognition and prestige. In the 1970s, under President Echeverría, who was born and raised in Mexico City, the country saw a rapid expansion of the social-security system in the provinces. Yet, like so many of our policies, this was temporary. Thus, as cabinet heads, we not only faced the frustration of contradictory programs within our own administration, but the lack of continuity in philosophy from one administration to the next.

The last few months of my administration presented few challenges. Some twelve months earlier, many of my colleagues had been engaged in the struggle for the presidency. As the events repeated themselves, the final candidate remained a well-kept secret. It eventually came down to a three-way struggle between the Secretary of the Treasury, the Secretary of the Presidency, and the Secretary of the Government. The latter, the late Gustavo Díaz Ordaz, won. He was a strong man, very moral. The people and the press never took to him the way they did to his predecessor. Many people had a false image of him, an image resulting from his harsh demeanor. He was not really like that. In fact, he was quite witty. He had a fine sense of humor and enjoyed telling jokes. The people who thought of him as cold did not really know him. I have always thought history misjudged him, as it is quick to judge many of us in public life. But, in my opinion, the judges were ignorant. The truth will eventually come out.

27

A Senator

I had no political connection with Gustavo Díaz Ordaz, our party's candidate for President in 1964. Nevertheless, because of my gubernatorial administration, the continued influence of Cárdenas in his home state, and the lobbying of President López Mateos with his successor, I was given the party's nomination for one of our two senate seats from Michoacán. Thus, I would end my political career as it had begun, representing my state in the Congress.

I easily trounced the opposition, which this time came only from PAN. Taking my seat in the Senate, I received an appointment as the senior Michoacán political figure to the Great Committee. Also, the President of the Senate asked me to serve on several committees, including labor affairs, constitutional affairs, and rules.

In Mexico, as any schoolchild knows, the Senate's role is very limited, confined to several duties well defined in the Constitution. My six years in that body normally would have passed without incident, a well-deserved respite after a long and arduous political career. The day-to-day activities in the

Senate are comparable to those in the Chamber of Deputies. A few distinctions in powers between the two bodies exist, the most notable being that the Chamber of Deputies has the exclusive right to approve the federal budget. My senatorial activities were reminiscent of my experiences as a deputy some twenty-five years earlier. However, we were a smaller and more cohesive body since no opposition party members were represented in the higher chamber. We did revise presidential legislation, and we introduced our own legislation, which had about the same chance of gaining approval as did laws proposed in the Chamber of Deputies.

It was rare for a senator to express publicly an opinion contrary to executive-initiated legislation. Such a posture would not be helpful to one's career, especially if you were at an early stage. However, many of my colleagues, like myself, were at the end of their careers, so, whereas their loyalties to the party were unquestionably strong, they were also more willing to express, however rarely, an independent position. But typically, on the chamber floor, our discussions were subdued and decorous. Rarely did our actions attract media attention. The events of 1968 changed all that, not that the confrontation between the students and the military was ever discussed publicly in our magnificent chamber. In fact, these events were only tangentially related to what took place.

For many years the Mexican army had not intervened so overtly, and with such force, in a political confrontation between the government and its critics as it did in September and October of 1968. To his credit, President Díaz Ordaz took full responsibility for the conflict's outcome. But the military itself received much criticism. To reward the Army for its loyalty, and to ensure its continued support of the political system, the President naturally increased the number of promotions from colonel to general. Constitutionally, the Senate must pass on all of these recommendations from the President. Within the Senate, the Committee on National Defense, normally made up of senators who themselves have been career military officers, recommends promotions to the larger body.

Soon after a list of individual recommendations arrived at the Senate, a yearly event, a senator and brigade general on leave from the service, who was a friend of my wife's father, stopped by to see me. He explained that the members of the committee were concerned about several of the promotions because they did not seem, in their view, to meet the requirements as specified in the law of promotion and compensation. He asked me as a senator and lawyer for assistance in finding some cases where our colleagues, in earlier sessions, had refused to approve presidential recommendations, a rare occurrence in recent years, especially since no opposition party members had been elected to the Senate. It seemed an interesting political and legal question and I offered to help.

I put some of my law office staff to work on reading through the Senate minutes dating back to the 1940s. After many weeks of work my staff encountered several cases in which the committee, and the full Senate, failed to ratify individual nominations. The first case where we found opposition to a promotion was not very helpful. Several senators in 1941 had questioned the promotion of an officer from brigadier to brigade general based on the belief that he had supported General Huerta against the Constitutionalists in 1913. But that officer's situation was not analogous to the present one, so it had to be discarded. However, in reviewing records from the 1940s and 1950s, we did encounter cases in which the Senate refused to approve several officers' promotions who, in the view of the National Defense Committee, hadn't served the proper time in grade and thus were ineligible for promotion.

Excited by these precedents, I took them to my colleague. I quoted from Article Seven of the promotion law, which stated. "Field-grade officers can be promoted to the immediate

higher grade after four years in rank at the present grade."
Delighted, he thanked me and added that he would need my
support on the Senate floor.

The following week the National Defense Committee refused to recommend two promotions from colonel to general.
My friend, the general, after asking for permission to speak as
a member of the Committee, had this to say: "Mr. President,
fellow Senators. I want to say to you that no member of our
committee has made this recommendation for personal reasons or reasons of revenge. All of us on the committee believe
that we are acting justly, and we have the conviction that there
will be peace, both in our conscience and our spirits, only if
there is justice."

He continued, "This recommendation, sirs, as you have
heard, relies on two fundamental points. First, there is a pa-
tent irregularity in these officers' military records. Both were
ordered promoted on September 16, 1966, and as you can com-
pute for yourselves, that time is too short to meet the require-
ment specified in the law of promotion for time in grade. As
the March 3, 1948 circular made clear, we have sought to eli-
minate favoritism in the promotion of general officers, and at
the very minimum, we have sought strict adhesion to the values and obligations in the law. These officers, if promoted,
will have passed through three ranks in less than six years.
How can we approve these promotions without paying attention to the many interested parties in the Army, men who have
given service in a patriotic and loyal fashion to the nation?"

The other senators present listened attentively to my colleague's exhortation, because a no vote on these promotions
contradicted the wishes of the President. Such a vote was a
bona fide rarity.

Another member of the committee, who sought to support
my friend, also asked for permission to speak. He argued,

"The case that we are considering is extremely important because the ranks of the Mexican army are saturated with generals and field officers for which there is no need. For an army of fifty thousand men we have too many generals, and as a consequence, if we continue to promote officers without following military rules, it will lead us to disaster."

Then, a most extraordinary intervention took place. One of my friends, Aquiles Represas, who had been a professor of law for more than four decades and was now a Supreme Court Justice, asked to speak. I considered him a courageous and eloquent public figure. A hush came over the Senate chamber. Represas began, "I believe that I have demonstrated perfectly clearly both to the press and before the court, that I am an active defender of the gravity of the Senate's responsibilities. When the Senate or its committees have found a discrepancy, it has been brought forth honestly and openly. No one can deny that the committees have worked hard, but they have received so many initiatives that a lack of time makes it difficult for them to give each of these questions sufficient attention. I would like to say publicly that I am a friend of one of the two officers in question, but I have never voted for friendship, I vote with the law. If his nomination is irregular, it should not be approved. This is all I ask."

This revelation was followed by tremendous applause.

The Secretary of the Senate then asked the assembled members if there had been sufficient discussion of the two cases. The senators replied in the affirmative. A senator interrupted, asking for an individual vote. The total vote was fifty in favor of the committee's recommendation, and one against. It was a vote for the law, for consistency, and for the institutionalization of our armed forces. It was my proudest day as a senator. If only we might have done it more frequently.

28

Retirement

I regularly go for breakfast and coffee at Sanborn's in San Angel where Insurgentes converges with Angel Quevedo Avenue across from the strange, austere monument to Obregón, which displays his severed arm like a valuable jewel. It is always crowded, but my friends and I enjoy our conversations there. Although my political career ended in 1970, occasionally some young friend or interviewer asks me about my retirement. One such interview occurred at the time I was writing these memoirs. The young man wondered what I had been doing since 1970.

I laughed, "As you can see, I sit here and make money as a lawyer."

He smiled, joining in my humor. "Seriously, though, how do you feel about ending your long service in government? With your experience, don't you have more to contribute?"

I explained to him that initially I had felt that way. When I talked with friends from my generation in the same position, I found many who were equally disenchanted with not having a responsible post. But that is how our system works. We do

211

not wish to make the same mistake as Porfirio Díaz, keeping one generation in power for too many years. The problem is that our reliance on personal loyalties is so strong that when our mentor leaves office, especially if he is the President, those identified with him must go to make room for others—usually younger men—who have stronger personal loyalties to his successor. If I were to be completely objective about it, I would argue that we have undervalued experience and skill and over-valued personal loyalty. We need to reverse the emphasis on these two characteristics. We aren't making use of the experienced talent available.

"But you're an advisor to the President, aren't you?" he asked.

"Yes, I am. Miguel de la Madrid was my student at the National School of Law. I'm honored that the President considers my opinion valuable. But many similar positions are only sinecures—temporary jobs with superficial prestige that are financial rewards to sustain a person from one administration to the next, when their fortunes might change. Many advisors do little or nothing to earn their salaries."

"I see. How do you explain why that continues?"

I answered frankly that it is an unwritten rule of political life here. In my opinion our government has become a bureaucracy, in the worst sense of the word. To sustain our government, we have made financial rewards more important than service. My generation wanted to serve the people. Of course, I don't deny some of us went into government because alternatives in private enterprise were limited, but we had service as an ideal. The political climate was different then. We had just undergone a major revolution, amidst which I grew up. This changed everything. At first, the uncouth, illiterate generals became our leaders. They governed crudely. But as my generation became educated, we found many positions of responsibility open to us. Leadership was needed because those who'd supported the *Porfiriato* were removed or abandoned their positions. Even many of the uneducated generals took educated men in their teens or twenties into their administration. The structures were changing, the laws were new. Alemán is a good example. His legal career in the post-revolutionary era was built on suits involving worker protection in the mines. If I recall correctly, his was the first thesis written on that subject at the National University.

The interviewer wanted to know more about my views on the bureaucracy.

"*Ay, hombre,*" I said. "You know Mexico City well. Look at all these buildings, these monstrosities. There's that new building for the Workers' Housing Institute, or the Foreign Trade Institute. Our revenues are being spent on buildings, not on the people. More bureaucrats. We fill these offices with government employees. That won't solve our problems."

"You mentioned an unwritten rule of Mexican politics. What exactly is that?"

"It's like social security," I said, "only we provide a special cushion for the politician. Politicians receive their security through long years of service and discipline. Not formally, of course, but by playing by the rules. We reward unquestioning discipline now. We don't examine service in a critical way. Service for whom? Self-service. That's what it is. The young *técnicos* don't speak up. They're not independent enough. Read that book by Díaz Ordaz's mistress, Irma Serrano," I recommended. "Now that is a woman who wears pants. Very gutsy, you know. The passage about Echeverría tying Díaz Ordaz's shoes for him after he leaves her bedroom is a classic case of servility. The man performs the services of a valet because he wants to become the next President. Where has pride gone?"

"I tend to agree with you, *Licenciado*. Are you saying that there's a generation gap?" asked my friend.

I wondered about a generation gap. There were some personal disappointments for me.

Part Five

"My son, Antonio, Jr., was a student leader in the 1968 movement. It was sad for me. I believe he lost sight of the issues and wasted a lot of time. He missed a semester because of his activities, and in the end I had to rescue him from the police. But don't misunderstand me. The government was wrong in its treatment of the students. The massive use of force was unnecessary. That was an internal political matter. But my son's generation has no self-discipline. I think we made a mistake with our children. We were too generous. Most of these students today come from middle-class families. Not like my background, or many of my companions. Success is too easy. They don't have to work for it."

I had put my young friend in an awkward position since he was about the same age as my son. But his reaction was diplomatic.

"Perhaps you're right. I see that happening in my own society. You've described several weaknesses in the present political system; how do you see the Mexican President and his role in the system?"

"Some of our intellectuals have recently expressed a view on that issue," I told him. "I assume you have read the books by the late Daniel Cosío Villegas. Don Daniel saw the President as an omnipotent power. I agree. One of my friends described the President as an absolute monarch. The stability of our political system relies heavily on his judgment and moderation. We've been very fortunate. Most presidents have not abused their authority, at least not in the extreme. But therein lies the weakness of our system. What if we have a President who lacks good judgment—the despotic monarch? You see, we don't have any institutional means of controlling him. There's nothing to stop him when he makes the wrong decision. Before it's corrected, it might be too late."

"And the other members of his administration, they can't help?" he asked.

"Yes, yes, they are one of the restraints. But as I said before, there aren't enough men of principle. They don't have the backbone of someone like Vasconcelos or Múgica. No, it's a serious weakness. Look what happened when President López Portillo nationalized the banks. He made that decision with the help of two individuals! The decision set back our relationship with the private sector three decades; but when the decision was announced publicly, how many of our leaders resigned in protest? Two, my young friend, only two."

"So you don't think too highly of these so-called technocrats?"

"It is an abused term. Overused. It conjures up different meanings to whomever expresses it. But yes, in general I share a distaste for the young technocrats. They are too self-assured. They believe their education provides the answer to every problem. Theoretically, the answer may be there. But politics is life. Politics is people. You don't learn that out of a book, especially one written by a North American. These people are overflowing with *theories*. They believe any problem can be administered away. Let me tell you my friend, I've learned from personal experience it isn't true. You have to know your own society's reality. Growing up in Mexico City is only one Mexico, a minority Mexico. But it's the Mexico that nurtures our leaders, molds their actions. We may have unintentionally generated an elite that is out of touch with the masses. If that is left uncorrected, we will face numerous problems."

Like many young scholars, he wanted to know if I thought Mexico was ready for a change, for the sort of mass participation that would lead to a democracy.

"A good question," I told him, "and a most difficult one to answer. We've had a violent history, with many uncompromising groups competing for their own interests. For example, look at the history of the clergy during the nineteenth century and after the Revolution. The behavior of these groups has made many politicians suspicious. Why? Because they lacked

215

the maturity and the responsibility to be good citizens. That's why we hesitated to give women the right to vote. Everyone thought they would vote for PAN, because of its conservatism and ties with the clergy. But, as you know, that didn't happen. Education has helped to change that. I think the Mexican people are becoming more responsible, they're taking their duties as citizens more seriously. But this isn't something that can happen overnight. We need to expand political participation, to involve more people, but this must evolve slowly and progressively."

My friend nodded in agreement as he wrote down my last sentence on his notepad. He thanked me for my time and frankness. We said our farewells until his next visit. Each year we met he seemed to get younger, like a fountain of youth, while I, seeing my oldest friends dying, aged more and more. Time to talk and think, yes; I have plenty of time. Mexico will change. I read about those changes in my parlor. I'm glad to have been part of my country's history. I'm not ashamed of what I have done. The future will tell if the younger generation can do as well.

Biographical Glossary

Alemán Valdés, Miguel. Son of General Miguel Alemán, he was born at the turn of the century in Sayula, Veracruz. He was Mexico's first president to graduate from the National School of Law and represented the famous 1929 generation. After briefly practicing law, he held several legal and judicial posts before being elected senator in 1934 and then governor in 1936 in his home state. General Avila Camacho, impressed with his abilities, tapped him as his national campaign manager in 1939, rewarding him with the post of government minister in his cabinet. Alemán was elected president in 1946 and is most remembered for his attempts to industrialize Mexico, both in agriculture and manufacturing. Although strongly criticized for the excessive corruption of his administration, Alemán produced the most important generation of politicians, who in terms of their ideological perspective, acted as a counterpoint to Cárdenas' disciples. He died in 1983, in charge of the National Tourism Commission, an agency he had directed since 1958.

Alessio Robles, Vito. A native of Coahuila and engineering graduate from the National Military College, Alessio Robles initially fought against Madero's supporters, served as military attaché to Italy, and

219

was imprisoned by Victoriano Huerta on his return to Mexico. He joined the Constitutionalists and later served as a federal deputy and senator from Coahuila. As president of the Anti-Reelectionist party, he opposed Calles and Obregón. In 1929, he was forced into exile. He wrote many books and became a prominent Mexican historian.

Almazán, Juan Andreu. Born in Puebla in 1891, the son of well-to-do landowners, Almazán left medical school when the Revolution started. Although he originally supported Madero, and then Zapata, he was allied with Huerta's forces against Carranza. In 1920, Obregón restored him to the regular army, where he became an important zone commander in Nuevo León. Almazán used his military position to promote a successful career in highway construction in northern Mexico. In 1939, he ran for president as the candidate of the Revolutionary Party of National Unification. After losing the election, he went into exile from 1940 to 1947. He died in 1965.

Andreu Almazán, Juan. See Almazán.

Avila Camacho, Manuel. Born in the same Puebla community as Vicente Lombardo Toledano in 1897, Avila Camacho pursued a career in the military beginning in 1914. He served as chief of staff under Cárdenas in Michoacán, and rose to the rank of general in 1924. Several times a military zone commander, he was subsequently *oficial mayor*, subsecretary, and secretary of defense from 1933 to 1939, when he resigned to accept the nomination of the official party for the presidency. He is remembered as a moderate, who among other achievements, toned down the state's confrontational attitude toward the Church.

Avila Camacho, Maximino. Brother of the president, Maximino was a cadet at the National Military College. He was a dominant political force in his home state, where he became governor in 1937. He joined his brother's cabinet in 1941 as Secretary of Public Works. Considered by many observers to be a power behind the throne, he

Glossary

was interested in controlling the presidency after 1946. His unexpected death in 1945 abruptly eliminated his political influence, including his opposition to Miguel Alemán as a potential successor to his brother.

Azuela Rivera, Salvador. Son of the famous novelist Mariano Azuela, Salvador attended school in various locations, including the National Preparatory School. Although Vasconcelos expelled him as a student leader in 1923, he supported his campaign for the presidency in 1929, organizing voters in Michoacán. A personal friend of Cárdenas, he is best remembered as a significant student orator and leader in 1929. He supported Almazán in 1940. He spent a lifetime in academic and intellectual activities and died in Mexico City in 1982.

Bassols, Narciso. Born at the turn of the century in the state of México, Bassols, similar to his co-disciple Gómez Morín, fostered an important generation of politicians and intellectuals. Dean of the Law School at thirty-one, Bassols served in numerous public posts at the state and national level, in a career that spanned three decades. In 1947, he founded the Popular Party, an antecedent to the moderately left-wing Popular Socialist Party. He is remembered for his integrity and for his stint as Secretary of Public Education from 1931 to 1934, during which he attempted to implement some of the more radical reforms favorable to socialist education. He died in 1959.

Beteta, Ramón. Born in Hermosillo, Sonora, in 1901, Beteta studied at the National Preparatory School and the University of Texas and completed his degree at the National University in 1926. One of the most important professors of Alemán's generation, he directed his campaign for the presidency in 1945. He held many posts in the federal bureaucracy, including Subsecretary of Foreign Affairs under Cárdenas, Subsecretary of the Treasury under Avila Camacho, and Secretary of the Treasury under Alemán. He produced a large pool of political disciples during his long career. He was a precandidate for president in 1951 and died in 1965.

Glossary

Calles, Plutaro Elías. A native of Guaymas, Sonora, Calles was orphaned at age four. Later he took the name of his stepfather. Like Múgica and many other revolutionaries, he taught school and also entered the field of journalism. He opposed the governor of his state and, in the initial years of Madero's government, held several local posts. Upon Madero's murder, Calles joined the Constitutionalists and rose to the position of military governor and commander of his home state. Later, in 1916, he served as the constitutional governor of Sonora, resigning this position in 1919 to join Carranza's cabinet. He left the cabinet in 1920 to support Obregón's presidential bid and later served as his Minister of Government. Calles succeeded Obregón in the presidency from 1924–1928. He is credited with many structural changes responsible for Mexico's present institutions, including the formation of the government party in 1929. He controlled Mexican politics after Obregón's death from 1929 to 1935, when Cárdenas eliminated his behind-the-scenes influence, exiling him to Los Angeles. He returned to Mexico in the early 1940s and died in 1945.

Carranza, Venustiano. Born in 1859, Carranza came from the northern state of Coahuila, one of the strongest seedbeds of the 1910 Revolution. During the Porfiriato, he served in many local and national political offices, including senator and interim governor. He joined the antireelectionist movement, and during Madero's presidency, served as governor of his home state. Upon Madero's death in 1913, he proclaimed himself first chief of the Constitutionalist Army, opposed to the government of Victoriano Huerta, and in favor of restoring the 1857 Constitution. General Alvaro Obregón commanded a major army under his direction. Although he convoked the Constitutional Convention of 1916–1917 when his armies were victorious, he did not sympathize with the radical provisions that emerged from that body. As President from 1916 to 1920, he followed a moderate course. Immediately before the 1920 presidential succession, he broke with Obregón, who, together with General Calles and others, overthrew his government. He was assassinated in 1920, fleeing to Veracruz.

Glossary

Casas Alemán, Fernando. A native of Veracruz, and a co-student with Ramón Beteta, Casas Alemán was a professor of the Alemán generation. He replaced his political mentor, Miguel Alemán (no relation) as governor of Veracruz from 1939–1940, following him into Avila Camacho's cabinet as Alemán's Subsecretary of Government. He also served as the head of the Federal District Department under Alemán. Many observers believe he was Aleman's personal choice to succeed him as president, but charges of excessive corruption during his administration in the Federal District sank his candidacy among other party and governmental leaders.

Caso, Antonio. A native of Mexico City, Caso was one of the leading intellectual figures in Mexico during the post-Revolutionary period. A teacher at the National University, who rose to the post of director of the National Preparatory School and rector of the National University, he influenced several generations of Mexicans with his thought. He was related through his brother to one of his intellectual opponents in the 1930s academic debates, Vicente Lombardo Toledano. His brother, Alfonso, served in the Alemán cabinet, and his nephew, Andrés, held important public offices in the 1970s and 1980s.

Castro Leal, Antonio. A member of Bassols's and Gómez Morín's generation at the law school, Castro Leal's public career is confined largely to the diplomatic corps. He briefly served as rector of the National University from 1928 to 1929. He is primarily remembered as an important literary critic and author. He died in 1981.

Elías Calles, Plutarco. See Calles.

Escudero, Juan. Son of a Spanish father and Mexican mother, Escudero founded a shipworkers union. He was affiliated with Ricardo Flores Magón, the famous Mexican precursor of the 1910 Revolution. Elected mayor of Acapulco in 1921, the police assaulted him in 1922 in the mayor's office. In 1923, when General Adolfo de la Huerta rebelled against President Obregón, he joined his forces. He and his brothers were captured and executed. He is remembered as a principled labor leader.

Gómez, Arnulfo R. A native of Navajoa, Sonora, Gómez participated in the famous Cananea mining strike in 1906, an event which produced many other prominent revolutionaries. He joined the Constitutionalists, fighting under Calles. Later, in the break between Obregón and Carranza, Gómez supported Obregón. He commanded the important military zone encompassing Mexico City under Obregón. In 1927, he opposed the reelection of Obregón. It has been debated whether he had little choice but to rebel, or already was committed to using arms against Obregón. He was caught in Veracruz and executed on November 4, 1927. Many of the students and intellectuals who supported his campaign against Obregón later supported José Vasconcelos in 1929. Members of that group were prominent among the political group of Miguel Alemán and Adolfo López Mateos.

Gómez Arias, Alejandro. Gómez Arias, similar to Salvador Azuela, was a prominent student at the National Preparatory and Law Schools in the 1920s. A leading orator for the 1929 Vasconcelos campaign, he helped Bassols found the Popular Party in 1947. He served as private secretary to Octavio Véjar Vázquez from 1942–43, but is best noted for his intellectual contributions as an independent essayist for various political magazines. He resides in Mexico City.

Gómez Morín, Manuel. Born in 1897, in a small town in Chihuahua, Gómez Morín began his studies in Catholic schools, and later completed his education at the National Preparatory and the Law Schools in Mexico City. His father, a miner, died when Gómez Morín was a young boy. A member of the important generation of 1915, Gómez Morín was a leading intellectual figure of his generation. As a professor, he recruited and influenced dozens of successful Mexican politicians, ironic because he was a leading figure in the establishment of Mexico's largest opposition party in 1939. The youngest Assistant Secretary of the Treasury in Mexican history, Gómez Morín

Glossary

was considered a financial wizard. He served as secretary and dean of the National Law School, and rector of the National University from 1933–1934. Abandoning the political establishment, he became an articulate opponent from the ideological right in the 1930s and 1940s. He also is a preeminent example of a politician who turned into a highly successful private-sector entrepreneur. His son, Juan Manuel, was an important force in the National Action Party in the 1970s. Gómez Morín died in 1972.

Lombardo Toledano, Vicente. A prominent labor leader born in Puebla in 1894, he was part of Gómez Morín's generation at the National School of Law. Lombardo Toledano began his career as a Christian Democratic and moved toward socialism in his later life. He held many university posts and founded and directed the Workers' University. Under Cárdenas, he headed Mexico's largest labor organization, the Mexican Federation of Labor. From 1948–1960 he was co-founder and president of the Popular Party with Bassols and others, and he died in 1968.

Leñero, Agustín. A Michoacán native and protegé of Lázaro Cárdenas when he was governor, he became his personal appointments secretary in 1939. He held a series of state and national positions, including numerous ambassadorial posts after 1940. Essentially, however, because of his close ties to Cárdenas, his upward political trajectory stopped in 1940.

López Mateos, Adolfo. He grew up in Atizapan, México, studying at private schools on a scholarship in Mexico City. He completed his studies in Toluca and at the National University. A student leader in 1929, he supported Vasconcelos for the presidency. The president of the National Revolutionary Party recruited him to the government in 1931. Elected senator of his home state in 1946, he was made secretary-general of the official party in 1951, a position he left to manage Ruiz Cortines's campaign for the presidency. Rewarded with the post of labor secretary, he skillfully managed labor relations during his administration and was rewarded with the presidential

225

nomination in 1958. One of the most personally popular presidents in recent history, López Mateos moved his government toward a more populist direction reminiscent of Cárdenas. He died in 1969.

Magaña, Gildardo. A native of Zamora, Michoacán, Magaña was a seminary student who later studied business in San Antonio, Texas. He fought under Emiliano Zapata, remaining in the army after the Revolution. He was appointed governor of Baja California in 1934 and was elected governor of his home state in 1936. An early candidate for the presidency in 1939, he died unexpectedly the same year.

Manrique, Aurelio. Manrique spent most of his boyhood in San Luis Potosí, although he completed normal school at the National University. He served under Obregón in the Revolution, and founded the National Agrarian Party in 1920. After serving as governor of his home state, he was reelected various times to the Chamber of Deputies. He earned a well-deserved reputation as one of the most outspoken and distinguished orators of his generation. He accused Calles publicly of complicity in Obregón's assassination. He died in 1967.

Morones, Luis. A native of Mexico City, Morones became one of Mexico's most influential labor leaders in the 1920s. He served in the Revolution with Carranza, and later supported Obregón. He founded the Regional Federation of Mexican Workers and ultimately served in Calles's cabinet as Secretary of Commerce. He opposed Obregón's reelection, but his own political influence came to an end when he remained loyal to Calles in his split with Cárdenas in 1935. Although he was partially successful in bringing a larger political role to labor, many Mexicans remember his labor leadership for its corruption and self-interest.

Múgica, Francisco J. Born in 1884, in Tinguindin, Michoacán, he grew up to be a schoolteacher. Later, he served as a local tax collector and entered the field of journalism. Attracted to politics, Múgica opposed the Díaz dictatorship. He moved to Mexico City in 1910 and then went north to join the movement sympathetic to Francisco Madero. In 1911, he participated in the first major battles of the Revolution. He rose up through the Revolutionary ranks to general and was a military governor and commander under the Constitutionalist forces in Tabasco in 1915. Elected a deputy to the Constitutional Convention of 1916–17, he is best remembered as a leading radical. He served as governor of Michoacán from 1920 to 1922, although he had to abandon the governorship because of differences with President Obregón. In 1934, he reentered the national political scene when Cárdenas appointed him to his first cabinet as Secretary of the Economy. In 1935, he took over the post of public works, where he remained until 1939. That same year he was a leading contender for President of Mexico. Years later, he campaigned for another presidential candidate in 1952 and died two years later.

Obregón, Alvaro. Born in 1880 in Siquisiva, Sonora, he worked in a mill and operated his own small farm. For a short time, he taught primary school. In 1911 he entered politics as mayor of Huatabampo. In 1912, he supported Madero against the rebellion of General Pascual Orozco. When Madero was murdered, he took up arms against General Huerta. He and Calles were early allies in state politics. Appointed chief of the Army of the North East by Carranza, he was victorious in many engagements. One of the most talented strategists of the Revolution, he remained loyal to Carranza when Francisco Villa opposed the government. In two decisive battles, he defeated Villa, losing his arm to an artillery shell. He returned to farming, but eventually led a rebellion against Carranza in 1920, successfully defeating government forces. Elected president in 1920, he instituted a more radical agrarian program than his predecessor. He successfully put down a rebellion in 1923, again involving the presidential succession. He antagonized many of his former supporters by reforming the 1917 Constitution to permit him legally to run for President in 1928. He won the presidency after a bitter and violent campaign. However, before taking office, he was assassinated by a religious fanatic. Some Mexicans believe Calles was responsible for his murder.

Glossary

Ortiz Rubio, Pascual. Born in 1877 in Morelia, Michoacán, Ortiz Rubio attended the same local school as did the fictitious Antonio Gutiérrez. Later, he completed his engineering degree in Mexico City. He entered local politics, serving as a federal deputy under the Madero government, before being imprisoned by Huerta in 1913. Governor of his home state from 1917 to 1920, he served in Obregón's cabinet. After Obregón's death in 1928 as president-elect, Ortiz Rubio became the official party's first presidential candidate. After defeating José Vasconcelos in a bitter presidential election, he served until 1932, when he resigned the presidency, the only elected president of Mexico since the Revolution to do so. His prestige suffered considerably because General Calles, without subtlety, controlled his government. Unable to tolerate Calles's interference in the sovereignty of the presidency, Ortiz Rubio resigned. Despite the problems in his political career, he made many contributions to his home state, and in his later life, was respected as an elder statesman.

Portes Gil, Emilio. Born in 1890 in Tamaulipas, Portes Gil graduated from the Free Law School in Mexico City. He served as a federal deputy from his home state three times, before being elected as governor. In 1928, congress appointed him provisional president after the death of Obregón, the youngest man to hold that office in this century. He served in the cabinets of Calles, Ortiz Rubio, and Abelardo Rodríguez, and was president of the official party from 1935 to 1936. He died in 1978.

Ruiz Cortines, Adolfo. Born in the port town of Veracruz in 1890, Ruiz Cortines never went beyond secondary school. A staff officer during the Revolution, he served as an aide to two prominent generals. After many bureaucratic posts, he rose to the position of *oficial mayor* of the Federal District, after which he became a federal deputy and governor from his home state. When Alemán's secretary of government died, Ruiz Cortines succeeded him in 1948, putting him in line for the presidency in 1952. One of the most politically savvy presidents in recent decades, Ruiz Cortines was respected for his integrity. He tempered the excesses of Alemán's administration during his presidency. He died in 1973.

Serrano, Francisco R. A native of Sinaloa, Serrano joined the Revolution at a young age, later becoming chief of staff to Obregón. Related through marriage to Obregón, he served as his subsecretary then Secretary of War. Under Calles, he headed the Federal District Department, before resigning to run for the presidency in 1927. Obregón was very fond of Serrano, originally treating him like a son. But believing his rebellion dangerous to his own presidential fortunes, and to Mexico's stability, he ordered General Fox to ambush Serrano's party and execute him on October 3, 1927.

Suárez, Eduardo. A native of Mexico, Suárez graduated from the National Preparatory School and the National University, where he taught law. He held numerous positions in the secretariat of foreign relations before Cárdenas appointed him as Secretary of the Treasury, a position he repeated under Avila Camacho. He was a mentor to many Mexicans in public finance. He died in 1976.

Torres Bodet, Jaime. Born in México City in 1902, Torres Bodet represents the Mexican intellectual who makes public life his career. A graduate of and professor at the National Law School, he served in many diplomatic posts before reaching the position of Subsecretary of Foreign Relations in 1940, and subsequently Secretary of Public Education three years later. Under Alemán he served as Secretary of Foreign Relations, and under López Mateos, he returned to the public education post. Founder of the Contemporáneos literary group in 1928, he was also an outstanding poet. Second only to Vasconcelos, he left the most complete memoirs of any Mexican politician. He committed suicide in 1974.

Vasconcelos, José. One of the most controversial figures in Mexican public life, Vasconcelos was born in Oaxaca, but lived in various parts of Mexico. His grandfather was a personal physician to Porfirio

Glossary

Díaz, but Vasconcelos was an early political opponent of his regime, after graduating from the National Law School in 1907. Although he served as rector of the National University and was considered a father figure to student generations, he never taught. Obregón, who respected his intellectual and revolutionary credentials, appointed him as the first Secretary of Public Education, where he had a profound influence on Mexican educational policy. Dismayed by some of Obregón's political decisions, he resigned to run for governor of his home state in 1923, but Obregón declared his opponent the winner. In exile under Calles, he founded an intellectual magazine to oppose his regime. Manuel Gómez Morín, among others, provided him with financial support during those years. He returned from Europe to conduct a presidential campaign in 1929, where he attracted student, intellectual, and middle-class support. Most objective observers believe that Vasconcelos may have won the urban vote, but not the majority of votes. Mercurial and dogmatic, Vasconcelos—to many Mexicans—would have made a poor president had he succeeded. In later life he disappointed many of his supporters with his sympathetic views toward fascism. His philosophic works are prominent in twentieth-century Latin American thought. He died in 1959.